Hey Trude!

The Life and Loves of a One-Time Sixties It Girl

Hey Trude!

The Life and Loves of a One-Time Sixties It Girl

TRUDIE WILLIS

Text Trudie Willis
Copyright © Trudie Willis

First print October 2023

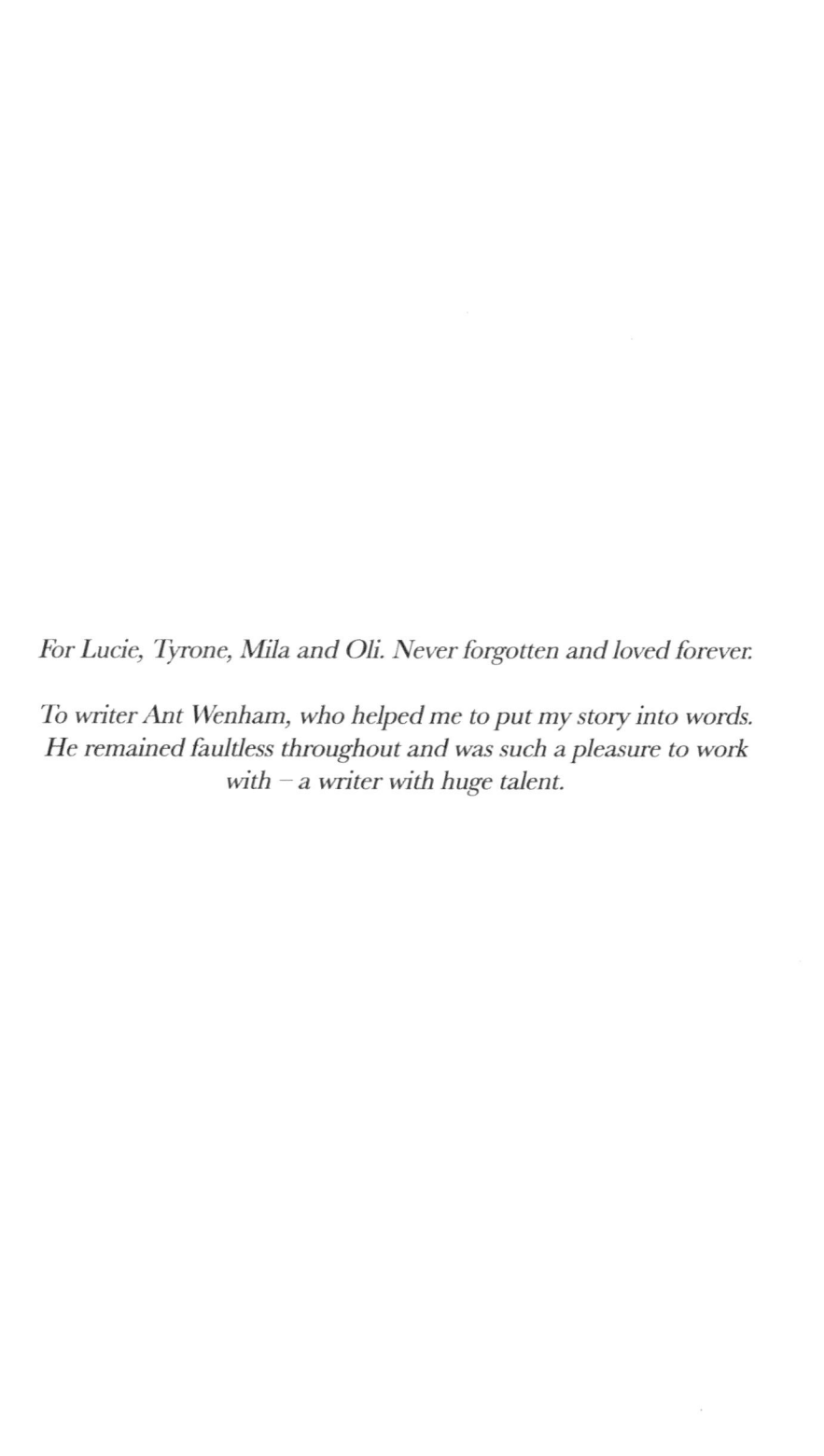

For Lucie, Tyrone, Mila and Oli. Never forgotten and loved forever.

To writer Ant Wenham, who helped me to put my story into words. He remained faultless throughout and was such a pleasure to work with – a writer with huge talent.

CONTENTS

CHAPTER 1	9
CHAPTER 2	23
CHAPTER 3	49
CHAPTER 4	57
CHAPTER 5	67
CHAPTER 6	77
CHAPTER 7	97
CHAPTER 8	113
CHAPTER 9	143
CHAPTER 10	161

CHAPTER 1

It's a question as old as time: 'Who is the father, my dear?' asked the rather stern gentleman. No doubt to his horror, and my mother's, I had to reply: 'I have no idea, I'm afraid.' Believe it or not, it was the right answer – and that was how I would become the last illegal abortion patient of Dr Eustace Chesser, an eminent Harley Street physician, who had lobbied Parliament for several years to end backstreet abortions and legalise and regulate the practice.

Naturally, I was a little shame-faced when I answered the doctor's leading question, but it did the trick. I was just 21, and the next thing I knew, there I was at 4 p.m., standing outside an imposing Victorian house in the east end of London. A friend had driven me there that afternoon. Holding my overnight bag, I knocked on the door and waited for an elderly maid to let me in.

How did it come to this? Well, dear reader, we have to go back a couple of years to find out how I came to find myself in the family way, supported by a very understanding mum. I am dyslexic, and so it was soon apparent that I was not going to attend Cambridge University as Daddy had planned. Nor would I go either to a finishing school in Geneva, a secretarial college in London, a nursing teaching hospital, or Lucy Clayton's modelling school.

Instead, I was sent to my last choice, the Eastbourne School of Domestic Economy, where I would learn how to run a household and find a suitable husband (by learning how to special-clean a loo, polish a ballcock, make French knickers and a hand-smocked Christening gown). Very useful, we were led to believe! Also, I learned high-class cookery and elementary catering and, above all, how to manage a household – once I had hooked that husband, of course.

On leaving Eastbourne, having completed the year and stayed on for another six months to complete the high-class cookery course, Aunty Vi, as we called her, who ran the Eastbourne school, found me a position as cook at the Villa Fondatore, owned by a couple called Michael and Jane Ryan, in St Paul's Bay, Malta. This was primarily a water ski school with a handful of rooms for visitors, where I was expected to cook three meals a day in exchange for free wine and five shillings (25p) a day! It was my proud boast, which my good friend James Sargant has often reminded me over successive years, that each week, I managed to serve up Instant Whip in seven different ways.

A brochure for the Villa boasted: 'Your food is prepared by a cook with high-class cooking and catering degrees, assisted by well-trained Maltese maids, who also do all the housework and laundry.'

St Paul's Bay is a village located along Malta's northern coastline. Traditionally, St Paul's Bay was known as a fisherman's village, although I'm told it's lost some of its character with the area's development as a popular tourist destination. The village's name refers to Saint Paul's shipwreck. According to the Bible, he was shipwrecked on an island while travelling from Caesarea to Rome, and folklore has it that this island was Malta. It is also believed that Saint Paul introduced Christianity to the Maltese. In the early 1960s, Malta was still a tranquil and idyllic island, basking in the Mediterranean sun. That period was Malta's halcyon day; these were the years before cheap flights brought over up to 400,000 tourists in a single month.

Life on my arrival in Malta in 1964 was a very different place from today. Food was usually fish (mostly tuna or swordfish), although the national dish was rabbit; each Saturday, families would congregate on the common above Madina to cook their rabbit and party. The only butcher on the island would unwisely show the hooves of his 'beef' animals; oddly, there seemed to be distinct donkey fur around those hooves, the chances of any beef being most unlikely! Also, on Saturday afternoons, just about every local car on the island got into a queue around the island and blew their horns non-stop.

Meanwhile, the poorer girls on the island would generally start work at age 13, and pay was almost non-existent. The courting of upper-class Maltese girls was very formal, with the daughters of the more class-conscious families kept largely out of sight or accompanied by both their parents.

How different from the experience of the English boys and girls of my acquaintance on the island… Each day, I got up at 6 a.m. to buy fruit from the passing grocer on his donkey and cart. Early errors included serving up a melon starter that proved to be a large pumpkin. A more exciting event occurred when I refused to buy some expensive snails, the reason being that I had spotted lots of snails climbing up the villa walls that same day after a rainstorm. I got our 13-year-old Maltese maid to collect them and place them in the only bath in the villa with a 'keep out' sign on the door. The poor bemused girl was instructed to feed the little molluscs with porridge oats and push them back into the bath if they crawled out. I then stewed up a generous portion, wiping off a rather revolting and constant froth in the process, and served them up with toothpicks and garlic butter. The unused creatures were oft found crawling back into the villa over the following days.

I told the mobile grocer what I'd done and gave him a rocket for trying to sell me over-priced produce that I could pull off the walls for free. He explained politely that his snails were special edible snails, specially imported from Italy, a wholly different and superior species to the garden snails found on the walls of my villa. Luckily, none of my guests died, apparently eating mine quite happily but completely ignorant of their provenance!

The second year I was in Malta was Independence Day, on 21st September 1964, when British rule ended. I was friendly with the then British Governor's two daughters, who were my own age (by now 20), as well as with a handful of young single WRENS working on the island for the Royal Navy at Hintafia.

For every visiting dignitary, arriving minesweeper, submarines from all over the world, plus the crew of the 6th fleet USA aircraft carrier (who had been on teetotal exercise for some months!), we would be summoned by the Governor to welcome each visiting ship along with all the official parties held at the Governor' Palace, or when requested by Borg Olivier, Maltese head of State at the time. So, together with friends at all the Army, Navy and Air Force bases, the parties never seemed to stop.

Once, I got an invite to the prestigious Naval Ball off the back of an unusual request. I knew Brush, the naval diver on Malta, and he had a consignment of naval cadets from Manaden due to go on a diving course off the island. I, in a happy drunken moment, said I would shave them all as a bet when they came back. They must have been very brave or stupid, but it got me the prized ticket to go to the big annual ball as their guest.

It should be remembered that Malta was a strictly Roman Catholic island, so much so that we would write to our prospective visitors to the villa advising them to bring no contraceptives or the newly developed birth control pill, which might be found by the assiduous Maltese Customs Officers, who would happily confiscate any such sexual contraband from incoming tourists. Helpfully, we used to suggest that our guests place any such items in a polybag and sink them into a jar of Brylcreem, the then-popular men's grooming product.

Sadly, my mother had failed to explain to me all the basics of sex and its consequences to me and had not put her ignorant daughter on the Pill. So, in hindsight, after two years of partying on a lovely Mediterranean island, surrounded by gorgeous men in uniform, it was probably no surprise that I would arrive back home for a party of 250 people invited to my 21st birthday on 23rd September 1965 to realise I had missed a period and was quite obviously pregnant.

I told no one at the time, but after the party, in floods of tears, I blurted out the news to my mum. In her usual way, she hugged me, told me not to worry and that she would sort it out – although no one in the family must know about it.

I have no idea where my mother found the £200 (worth almost £5,000 today) required to pay for it. She had taken me to Harley Street, where I met Dr Chesser and was interviewed about having a termination. I remember that there was one other mother and a young girl there, too. After the interview, we were sent to another Harley Street address, where a psychiatrist quizzed us to ascertain if a termination was appropriate. We then went back to Dr Chesser, where the other girl was leaving in tears, presumably having been refused on psychological grounds.

Inside were three camp beds. I was told to get undressed, and then the maid would bring me a nice cup of tea. She told me I was to stay put, and a gentleman would arrive, put me to sleep, and she would be there with another cup of tea ready to be picked up by my mum and taken home – no longer pregnant – the following morning. It must have happened exactly as she'd said, as I was collected by mum, who told the family I had a bad attack of flu, and she was putting me to bed for a few days in order to recover.

To this day, I have absolutely no memory of what happened to me in that East End house. And thus began the '60s for a young blonde girl from Essex.

Uncle Roy toasts me on my 21st birthday whilst I was secretly pregnant, Mummy on the left.

Local reaction to the Brits' beachwear (see right).

Cause of all the fuss; That's me lying on the ground!

Portrait by Bob Trotter, from my Maltese license photo.

Taking it easy between parties in Malta.

Villa Fondatore, my Malta base.

Shaving the divers in Comino, earning me a ticket to the ball.

Making the most of the facilities, water-skiing off Malta.

CHAPTER 2

My entrance into this world came with a big bang! The Second World War was in its closing months in the autumn of 1944, and at this time, the Germans had had their doodlebug positions pushed back further into France so that they were no longer able to target London. As a result, they would let them go at random.

When a woman was due to give birth in those days, a midwife would move in for a month to oversee the procedure. It so happened that my mother had employed a nurse who had just come from the famous actor Sir John Mills' family, whose son had been born in their house outside Felixstowe. As my arrival approached, the midwife recognised the sound of an approaching doodlebug, drew the blackouts and waited.

They came flying low over our house in Great Yeldham on the Essex-Suffolk border, no doubt in search of the nearby American base, where, incidentally, my mother ran the mess bar. The doodlebug came close enough to take several of our roof tiles off during my critical arrival. From that moment onwards, I have hated loud bangs, from having to be removed from the Bertram Mills circus when the exploding clown's car arrived to having to listen to fireworks from the safety of a bedroom window.

The next day I began to bond with Dick, who would become my lifelong friend. The day after I was born, he turned up at the house with a posse of workers to mend the roof, But he wisely reckoned that a wet and cold trip to the roof was a no-show. Instead, he offered to push the new baby around in her pram, and so began a long friendship.

Dick was then employed making Nissen huts for Whitlock Bros during the war; later, he applied for and got the job as my father's gamekeeper, and it was from Dick that I learned the rules of the countryside from a hut in the woods, where he reared the game and dangled dead predators from a rope outside the building.

His gamekeeping days lasted until my father died, after which he became Lord Sainsbury's gardener, and I am happy to report that the kind Lord Sainsbury unknowingly kept me in free vegetables for several years. Dick went on to run the local pub, load for an array of famous shooters, become a local raconteur and know everyone from poachers to peers.

I had a happy childhood. My first memory was gazing up out of my pram to see the berries hanging off the yew tree under which I would be deposited every afternoon in the spring and summer. I wasn't to know until later, but there had been another baby, Sally, after my brother Nevil and before me, but so sadly, she had been a cot death at eight months – so hard for Mummy and Daddy. Sally is buried in the churchyard at Gt Yeldham, along with my grandparents, great uncle, daddy, Uncle Roy and his wife Jill.

Like so many of us, as we get older, I remember long, hot summers, lawnmowers buzzing and endless butterfly hunts. I don't recall much about the winters except that the house was cold and a little eerie (perhaps because of the animal heads mounted on the walls!), I remember roller skating in the hall and boxing sessions with my brother Nevil (which usually ended with me in floods of tears and me lying to Mummy, 'But I like it' because I didn't want my brother to get in trouble).

Christmas was special, of course, with a big tree and presents. But, for me, the highlight was always the Christmas Eve shoot, which involved raucous parties of ruddy-faced, plus-foured shooters, downing port, whisky and Stilton cheese, all consumed in a haze of cigar smoke. Nevil and I were allowed to attend until the stories became a little too adult!

One Christmas stands out when we had a chimney fire, and the Fire Brigade had to come out, and then there was the January when we lost three grandparents and uncle and a family friend, Sheila Nicholls, all in the space of a few days. Lots of talking in whispers and Mummy crying, something we never expected grown-ups to do.

I went to school at St Margaret's, at nearby Gosfield, until I was 11. I was happy there, if not unduly intelligent. I remember hating it when Nevil went away to prep school at Orwell Park, near Ipswich. But we had Helen Harper to look after us until I was 11, someone who was among my most loved people along with Mummy, Daddy and Nevil.

I spent a lot of my childhood with daddy's farming friends in Gestingthorpe, a place where I liked to stay as often as possible as their house had every last comfort from warm carpets to delicious food. Here, I experienced my first stainless glass basins, impromptu parties, and my first oyster – which would be rapidly spat out across the table by me. Anne, their daughter, was three years older than me, but we played happily in the barns, dressing up their dogs, finding kittens, and just being children until Anne's hormones started kicking in!

Strangely, Ann's mother (Aunty Helen) and my mum were both Helen's, while confusingly, a third Helen, Helen Harper, looked after me and Nevil! Mummy would ring Aunty Helen daily on Hedingham 75, and the operator would say, 'Hello, Mrs W is having her hair done and will call you later'!

Later, when I moved to Sheepcotes, Aunty Helen designed my room like her daughter's – full of soft colours, a covered dressing table and special curtains and carpets. I was in heaven. Mummy's good taste related to her clothes only!

And did those two Helens know how to shop! To such an extent that Nevil and I would often be plonked into one of London's many newsreel short film cinemas as they hit the city; alternatively, we children were put under the charge of an usherette, while Harrods, all the top shops, and especially a row of unusual Jewish boutiques were hunted through for the latest trends. We youngsters often spent most of the day in the cinema.

Aunty Helen had a long room with a huge oak table and an open fireplace at each end. If there was a party, they would roll back the carpet for the night, and there would be dancing. One night, Aunty Helen was warming her bottom in front of the fire and suddenly blurted out: 'Oh Basil [my uncle], I can feel those wicket-keeping hands all over me! In fact, it was a large gladioli from a vase of fireside flowers that had found its unwelcome way to my aunt's rear end!

And it was Aunty Helen who, way back in the 1960s when she was in her eighties (as old as I am now) told me about B fuckyoume latta. We were looking at plants, and she said to me: 'You know people are always asking me about such and such a plant is called and, not having a clue, I always look them firmly in the eye and tell them, 'It's B Fuckyoume latta,' and I find they tend not to bother you again!

This is not a gambit that I would ever employ with my open garden visitors (who often know more about the plants than I), but 80 years on, I do wonder how many people have asked a puzzled nursey worker if they have any B fuckyoume latta. I certainly haven't helped by passing on the story many times. Thanks, Aunty Helen!

Before we go on to my time at boarding school from 11 to 15, I must reveal a little about my family and tell some of the stories of my amazing grandfathers and uncles.

My mother, Helen Mills, was born in Norwich, the second youngest in a family of five. Her father and uncle were eminent doctors in the city, and the family had a beautiful thatched weekend cottage on Ranworth Broad with four acres of land. The village's church of St Helens has a stained glass window in it and silver offertory plates donated by the family, and many of my family are buried in the graveyard.

In Norwich, my grandfather and his brother practised in partnership until they fell out after more than 40 years together. Uncle James would die at the age of 94 in the 1950s, still with a full private practice and believed to be the oldest and longest-serving doctor in the country. In his early twenties, his father had sent him on a cruise ship to Ceylon as the shipboard doctor to gain experience. At the same time, he was asked by Royal Kew Gardens to collect the first rubber trees to be planted in Ceylon, now Sri Lanka. He nursed them carefully in his dispensary and delivered them to Ceylon's botanic gardens. Subsequently, I had the pleasure of seeing where the remains of that first tree was planted.

The Mills lived in a large house on Surrey Street with a big garden, which now forms part of Norwich Bus Station! The next-door neighbour was John Colman of mustard fame. One memorable day, my grandfather surprised my mother by taking out her tonsils on the kitchen table; Mummy also recalls him keeping a large glass jar in the house to demonstrate to everyone his latest recurring kidney stone. He was born in 1874 and served as a major in the Royal Army Medical Corps during the First World War. Among his patients was the famous British painter Sir Alexander Munnings, who, it's believed, gifted some of his paintings, which hung above the fireplace on Surrey Street.

We thought we partied, but I'm pretty sure my mum must have outdone me! In her teens, she would drive her father around Norwich on his rounds to earn pocket money, which she put to good use. Never one to sit on her laurels, she found her own excitements, not to mention boyfriends.

She went on the books at Marshall's flying school in Cambridge and learnt to fly Tiger Moths, looping the loop effortlessly. At night, she might be found at the Theatre Royal or the Maddermarket Theatre, where she recalled performing at least two leading roles. The Broads and Lowestoft Sailing Club also featured in her busy life. Mummy is remembered by many for her now infamous spring catchphrase, "Hooray, hooray, the 1st of May, outdoor fucking starts today!"

Even at the fine age of 96, the 1st of May did not pass her by unnoticed, much to the alarm of her care home staff as she regaled all and sundry with her happy saying.

She nearly married Bobby Bond of the famous Bond's Store in Norwich (now John Lewis), she was both an excellent swimmer and sailor of boats, could ride to hounds and, I'm not really sure how, but she also found time to sell rare Swallowtail caterpillars on the market for a penny each.

What I enjoyed most was the way they partied. I just loved the idea of their games: a sheet would be hung up along the sitting room, and the ladies would gather behind it in the dark; the aim was simply to feel the ladies and guess who they were! Sometimes, they played by passing an orange around with only the use of their chin. Then, the really revolting one – the floor was crisscrossed with string; you put an end in your mouth, chewed your way up the string – and then kissed whoever you met in the middle! Apparently, if you didn't fancy the man at the other end, you had to quickly backtrack, spitting out your string whilst the eager pursuer at the other end chewed faster on your now soggy string to claim their kiss!

Sometimes, Mummy told me, she would have to use her precious pocket money to clean up an evening dress that she had been sick on. And we thought we knew how to party!!

All this would come to an end, however, when she met the woman who was to become my Aunt Sylvia and was introduced to her dashing brother, Carlton Whitlock. And so my father came on the scene.

At about this time, Mummy's sister, Aunty Betty, departed for Kenya and married my Norwegian uncle. He had lost his wife to tsetse fever, leaving him with three children aged under six. They settled at his sawmill in Nanyuki during the Mau Mau outbreak. Earlier, my uncle Peter had become bored in Norwich and set out to join them. There, he joined the Kenyan police and was promoted to Assistant Head of the British High Commission, all while the Mau Mau uprising was at its height.

The uprising is now regarded as one of the most significant steps towards a Kenya free from British rule. The Mau Mau fighters were mainly drawn from Kenya's major ethnic grouping, the Kikuyu. More than a million strong, by the start of the 1950s, the Kikuyu had been increasingly economically marginalised as years of white settler expansion ate away at their land holdings.

Since 1945, nationalists like Jomo Kenyatta of the Kenya African Union (KAU) had been pressing the British government in vain for political rights and land reforms, with valuable holdings in the cooler Highlands to be redistributed to African owners. Radical activists within the KAU set up a splinter group and organised a more militant kind of nationalism. By 1952, Kikuyu fighters, along with some Embu and Meru recruits, were attacking political opponents, raiding white settler farms and destroying livestock.

In October 1952, the British declared a state of emergency and began moving army reinforcements into Kenya. So began an aggressively fought counter-insurgency, which lasted until 1960 when the state of emergency was ended.

Sadly, Auntie Betty and Arthur were forced to leave when their house boy was told by the Mau Mau to kill them or be killed himself if he failed. Peter went back to Ranworth Broad a few years later, where he owned the moorings and shooting rights. He was a quiet, very good-looking man who lived happily with Barbara, his much younger East End second wife.

On the other side of the fence was my great-grandfather on my father's side, the Whitlock family. He owned 1,000 acres of land, employed 70 people and was an early champion of the Suffolk breed of sheep, winning The Presidents Cup in 1889. He also kept a private herd of black sheep from which his carpets and overcoats were made. His 1,000 acres was down to grass forage, which was shipped out to feed the horses in the Boer War in South Africa.

My grandfather, Thomas Whitlock, would go on to start Whitlock Brothers with his brother Herbert. He also became a long-standing churchwarden and loving grandfather to me. I adored him, with his vast productive garden, lawns, bowls, croquet lawns and rows of beehives.

The company was established in 1899 as Whitlock Brothers and gradually expanded to include foundry and carpentry shops. All types of agricultural machinery, wagons, carts and trailers, together with a variety of wooden buildings, were supplied. In 1941, Whitlock Bros Ltd was incorporated, and my father Carleton, having joined the company in 1924 aged

18, became chairman and managing director, and the company began to diversify into earth-moving machinery.

The Whitlock Dinkum Digger, a backhoe attachment for Fordson and Ferguson tractors, was the first tractor-mounted hydraulic excavator-loader, thus beginning a category of machines now colloquially referred to as JCBs, amazingly Whitlocks manufactured their prototype some two years before JCB or any other competitor. This was followed by the first hydraulic dredger, known as the Whitlock Dinkum Dredger, for clearing rivers and canals and what was then the largest hydraulic drill rig in the world. In 1960, the first Dinkum Dumpers were built, followed in 1963 by Britain's first hydrostatic dumpers.

The name of Whitlock was synonymous with earth-moving equipment and became known around the world. Sadly, Whitlocks was taken over in 1972 by Powell Duffryn, owner of the Hymac company, for £1.2 million. All Whitlock manufacturing was moved to the Hymac factory at Rhymney in Wales in the mid-1970s, and the Gt Yeldham site was taken over by a new Volvo UK operation. A subsidiary Whitlock company in Australia was established, with a network of distributors in many countries.

When Daddy joined the company, there were 12 employees on the payroll. At the time of his death in 1966, there were almost 600 employed at the Gt Yeldham factory. In that time, my father (or AC, as he was known) would be made OBE for services to exports and industry in 1963, as well as becoming a Royal Warrant Holder as the supplier of agricultural machinery to the Queen in 1955. He travelled extensively on business, visiting India, Africa, North America and all over Europe.

I was enthralled by the factory, which Nevil and I would tour with Daddy on Sunday mornings. First, we would go into the assembly shop to see the pristine new machines shining on the shop floor. No climbing over these beauties for us children. Next, we headed across to the paint shop, a place of wonder to me with its vast vats of blue or red paint, where whole trailers could be dunked to emerge seconds later in brand-new livery.

From here, we would go into my father's favourite place, the machine shop, where every new machine would be tested thoroughly. This was never a popular destination for me – it stank of oil, dirt and grime – but it fascinated Nevil and Daddy. From here to the stores where it was my job to empty the suggestions box, an innovation that Daddy sometimes found very useful, and he would often take up the ideas.

Surprisingly, one day, I found a French letter in the suggestions box, a practical joke by one of the staff. I'm sure Daddy felt it would be of little use to him; for myself it was treasure. I thought I had found a funny balloon!

Finally, we would make our way to the offices, where Daddy would linger over the drawing boards, checking any new designs, while I sharpened all the pencils that I could find. I wondered if the staff coming in on Monday mornings believed there must be a pencil fairy in the area! Tour over, Nevil and I would walk home to get cleaned up as Daddy headed off to the White Hart for a lunchtime pint.

As a young man, Daddy helped to set up Sudbury Rugby Club and was a playing member of Colchester and Rosslyn Park RFCs. He was also capped several times for Eastern Counties Rugby. Latterly, he was president of Gt Yeldham Football Club. He adored shooting and fishing, with shoots in the Gt Yeldham area and at Six Mile Bottom, near Newmarket, and a holiday cottage in Herefordshire where he had fishing rights on a mile beat of the River Wye.

At 11, my parents were to divorce, and I would depart to a boarding school across the Thames that didn't require an 11-plus, so Lillesden in Hawkhurst, Kent, became my home from home for the next five years. When Mummy and Daddy told me that they were divorcing, amazingly, I replied: 'I know'. Actually, I didn't, but it didn't hit me too hard, just the odd tears at Lillesden (often when it was to my advantage at school).

The school was set in beautiful grounds, with rhododendrons and azaleas all around. The junior school had been the home of Lord Collingwood, an admiral in the Napoleonic Wars and friend of Lord Nelson, and those gardens were lovely, too. Well, gardens are one thing, but behind the gates were a lot of restless girls longing for freedom and excitement.

The school's facilities were archaic, to say the least, and the headmistress was a five-foot, 20-stone Cambridge academic who could levitate and lived with her female companion, ensuring no male should ever open the gates.

You began on the top floor where ten girls would have access to two ewers (big jugs), in which they either cleaned their teeth or washed before one poor girl would be detailed to carry the 'slop bucket' down to the loo and empty it.

At 11, I was the oldest by a year, bottom of the class with little desire for an education and a great intent to write to as many male boarding schoolboys as possible; having a brother and two stepbrothers, this proved relatively easy.

While my friends seemed to be expelled on a regular basis (my best friends were Michaela Marson and Sally Hill, both removed before their time), I somehow never got caught in my misdemeanours. At 12, on a wildlife walk, my two friends and I (sadly, Sally was the prudish daughter of a vicar) were most excited to discover a prostrate naked man, believed to be from the nearby Russian rest home; he was wielding an axe while hiding in a hedge. The police became involved, and the school authorities were so upset that we were never allowed out alone again.

When I was 13, I went on a regular swim in the algae-laden, misty swimming pool – big enough for eight people and quite revolting – I picked up jaundice and spent a wonderful term concealed in my Coggeshall bedroom with Top of the Pops, my guitar, and meals of steamed chicken and fish – with schoolbooks stashed out of the way under my bed I was perfectly happy, despite the fact no one could see me as I was infectious!

I had now moved to Sheepcotes in Coggeshall, where my mother had married John Nicholls, a very loving and fun stepfather. He was a seed merchant in Coggeshall with John K King & Sons. Daddy later married Nancy, who we liked but who never really made much impact on Nevil or me. Now I was sharing the house with Nevil and Francis and Mark, my two stepbrothers, and from then on, all friends (other than a small handful of true girlfriends) were to be male.

Every year, John piled us into his huge Jags and rolled us down to France, the Balearic Isles or the Costa Brava, even a nudist island off La Lavendou. I returned at 13, having secured marriage proposals from a Spanish waiter, a Barcelona football player and a nightclub guitarist as my poor stepfather topped up his gin glass while the boys egged me on! I well remember the poem I wrote that year in the term while I mourned my latest lost love, secretly relieved at holding on to a very fragile virginity! This was to one Kim Carcasonna (where is he now?).

'Nature continually says goodbye as flowers bloom and flowers die,

People come, and people go, as happiness goes hand in hand with woe,

Alas, but one thing stays: it is my love for you that still remains,

Untouched and undisturbed, it must wait until I perish.'

Although boarding school was not an unhappy time for me, I did suffer from homesickness, was undoubtedly dyslexic and bottom of the class, as well as possessing two left feet whenever sport was involved. I did manage two O-levels: Geography and English Literature (although I never could spell), and even these two passes remain a mystery.

At 15, I was the youngest girl to become a prefect in the fifth form before a somewhat exasperated father took me out of school to enter the Eastbourne School of Domestic

Economy, where I would learn to run a house and the suitable husband when he could be found!

Sally joined me at Eastbourne, where we learned everything anyone would want to know about cleaning, sewing, smocking and dress-making. And cooking, of course, which I was good at and enjoyed thoroughly, leaving the college with glowing references.

Eastbourne was largely about growing up: life was up in the clouds or down in the dumps. Outside the classroom or kitchen, we would experiment with green nail polish, outrageous hats (I remember one green bowler with a veil), Black Russian cigarettes and crème de menthe and gin. Oh, and I managed unintentionally to lose my virginity. It was on a skiing holiday that Nevil had organised in Switzerland and, in the best traditions, was not a happy experience. The man, I think, was Polish and certainly nearer 40 than 30. I genuinely didn't know what he was doing, and after (for me) an anti-climactic conclusion, he became very cross when it became clear that I was a virgin. In my innocence, I thought I'd wet the bed! Obviously, it didn't put me off, but it was a bad start.

My first boyfriend on the Eastbourne scene was an Eastbourne College graduate who had access to his mother's small Mini. It took another 50 years for that relationship to be consummated! We did have a stab at it in the early days when he was living on a London barge. He invited me to meet up at a B&B for the night. I'm not so sure the landlady was aware of my presence or if my stay had been paid for. Anyway, the room was minuscule and surrounded by holy crucifixes on every wall; we lay inert and spooked, and no action took place. So roll on 50 years, and advice to one and all not to give up. He was a truly talented artist with a flair for the music of my era, as well as a good friend.

After three terms at Eastbourne, run by 'Aunty Vi' as she was affectionately known, Sally left while I stayed on to complete the haute cuisine course. Later, I discovered that shy, conservative Sally would go on to have an abortion, join the Communist Party and work in social services (later marrying her supervisor) in a role mainly involving the transport of East End prostitutes to the VD clinic.

Anyway, after 18 months at college, I was ready to go out into the wide world, a place that seemed full of promise to a 17-year-old blonde full of optimism and a sense of adventure.

Me in the lovely gardens at The Grove.

Mummy's party trick, balancing a bottle on her head at Ranworth Broad, Norfolk.

Me, Daddy, Nancy and Nevil at Daddy's OBE investiture.

Butter wouldn't melt... a new term starts at Hill House.

High kicks for a young me, rehearsing the can-can.

Me and best friend Sally Hill at Lillesden.

Sweet sixteen, me with Daddy at a party.

Me with stepfather John.

Mummy and John on holiday in the Bahamas.

CHAPTER 3

I was heading to a job interview with a then five-star hotel as a cook – but I never got there! After I left Eastbourne, I was going with my brother Nevil for the interview when we stopped along the way for lunch at the Bull Inn at Nettlebed. I never looked back because here we discovered the landlord, David Evans.

David was a ruddy-faced, monocled, larger-than-life commander of a two-man submarine in the Second World War who rose to the rank of admiral. At the time, he contracted malaria and would nearly die later when his annual attacks left him sweating and shaking for three days non-stop. Strangely, he had worked briefly for Daddy after the War, but this only came to light later.

A true Irish Catholic, he could also speak and sing in Welsh, consume two cases of bottled Guinness a day, often with a red-hot poker inserted into them, followed by several fine malts around the fire after closing hours – although, in fact, he would say that we never closed! As a coaching inn, as long as one of the drinkers signed in as a guest each evening, somehow, that entitled everyone, including the local policeman, to drink legally all night. Often our customers came down after hours from London and Henley.

It was all such fun; I decided this place looked a lot more entertaining than where I had been heading.

David's best friend was the then Abbot of Belmont, near Oxford, and the nicest man you could wish to meet. He was a good friend of the Pope and would stay with us on his way to Heathrow for his frequent visits to the Vatican in Rome. I remember the abbot had a new young priest who he felt was unsuitable for the monastery, so he sent him to us to restore an old painting in the dining room, encouraging us to get him in the bar to enjoy the secular life. It worked, and he withdrew from the priesthood.

Meanwhile, on Sundays, because there was nowhere for a local mass, David would invite the priest every Sunday at 10 a.m. into a very smoky, alcohol-scented saloon bar from the night before (not a pretty sight or aroma) to perform the service. Afterwards, I would join him for oysters and Guinness before the pub opened officially at noon.

His lovely wife suffered him and barely appeared while looking after their three daughters, the youngest of whom I remember was a friend of Marianne Faithful, at the time Mick Jagger's girlfriend.

David was an ardent rugby fan, and I clearly remember the Welsh international team stopping off at the Bull on their way to play England at Twickenham. The team arrived by coach early in the morning and were offloaded at the inn. We served them huge steaks while the coach set off for Henley, a couple of miles down the road, where the team would jog to rejoin it. And so on to Twickers. How times have changed since the amateur game.

These were troubled times in Ireland, and Catholics and Protestants rarely mixed. One year, however, a mixed police team of both religions arrived to take part in the Henley Regatta. Frankly, the rowing was subsidiary to another hobby – drinking! We put them at the Bull, where the Guinness on tap proved a great crowd-pleaser, with the first rower of one religion to pass out, footing the evening's bill for the other 'worshippers'.

There are many lovely pub stories from this time; outside of London, it was one of the places to be in the 1960s. Travel writer Peter Fleming, brother of Ian, the James Bond author, lived round the corner along with the actor Robert Morley, whose son I sometimes went out with. Robert told a lovely story of travelling in his chauffeur-driven Rolls up the Mall when a little old lady drove into the back of the car. He heard her say to the chauffeur: 'That's not like me, I've been driving for years.' Down came Mr Morley's car door window, and he replied: 'Well then, madam, you must be very tired.'

There are so many funny stories from this time, and here is a selection of the funny incidents that happened to me while I was at The Bull that I must include.

Every week, David or I put an advert in the Reading Times. On this occasion, a gentleman rang and spoke to me. He said sadly he didn't have a wife, but would it be all right if he booked a table and brought his young Jersey cow along with him! I went a little quiet until he suggested he read our advert in the Reading Mercury that week. We had written: 'Give your wife a treat and bring her to the Nettlebed Bull.'

By now, I had a car, and on one of my days off, I got dolled up and headed into Reading to catch the train for a night out on the town with friends. As ever, I was running late for the train and stopped a passing policeman to ask where I might drop off my Mini for the night. He kindly pointed me towards a lorry park near the station. I found the empty park, drove in, dumped my car and ran for the train.

Fast-forward to early morning when I got the train back and went to pick up my Mini. Could I have got it wrong yet again? As I approached my car, from the noise, it became apparent that I had mistaken the cattle market for the lorry park. There, in the middle of the pens, was my little red Mini, with hurdles around it, the auctioneer with his papers across the roof of my car, and a handful of sheep in the ring on offer to surrounding farmers. Quietly (in my best overnight Susan Small suit), I explained my predicament. The next thing I knew, myself and the car were being put up open to offers! I was finally released, and the Reading Mercury had a rib-tickling story for the next day's edition!

Often, when I went up to London for the night, I would leave my Mini at the Anglers in Egham and get a lift back the next day in time to get back to the pub for the official opening time. The Anglers had a circular drive with ornamental gas lamps all around. As ever, on my return from London, my mind was on other things, so when I put my foot on the accelerator, I was in first gear instead of reverse.

All this was playing out opposite the restaurant's low-level kitchen windows, and as I drove absent-mindedly into the lamp post, the Italian cooks raced out, picked my Mini up – with me inside it – and sent me on my way. I did, however, receive a bill to replace the gas light and lamp post. How do I do these things? Easily!

Goldy was a golden Eagle who escaped from the London Zoo for 12 days in 1965. At the time, I was going out with a reporter from the Daily Express, who lived in Didcot. He came into the bar and said he was at a loss because they'd caught Goldy. He had no story, so, in my usual helpful way, I said he'd better put me in the paper instead! 'Alright,' he said, 'jump in my car, I've got an idea.'

So off we went and found a farm gate that I swung over while he snapped me. Alas! The next day, the picture appeared in the William Hickey column, with a caption that read: 'Wealthy industrialist's daughter' (naming my father and the Whitlock company). This, in turn, appeared alongside a column headlined 'Long-legged, empty-headed debs'. That morning, I received a telegram from my father advising me that my monthly clothing allowance would cease immediately if anything like that appeared again!

Speaking of clothes, one day, I drove into Henley with the one aim of taking my red skirt to be dry-cleaned. Imagine my irritation when I got back and realised I'd left it behind. Then, about two nights later, I sensed an atmosphere in the public bar – you know, when you feel that everybody is in on a secret except you. At last, the oldest of the locals piped up in a voice that could be heard through the pub: 'Did you have a good night last evening, Trudie?'

Coolly, I replied: 'Thank you, Jack. Yes, I did.' But, wracking my brains, I couldn't think of anything untoward that might have happened the night before. It began to annoy me, so I cornered Jack and demanded to know what I might have done to cause such local interest. 'Nothing really,' he said. ' It's just that your red skirt has been hanging off the bushes on the main road by the wood.'

And so began and ended the short-lived legend of the rape of Nettlebed. I'm not sure any of them believed me, but I tried to explain that I must have put the skirt on the roof of my car before leaving for Henley, and it must have blown off onto the bushes on the way home. The locals were not convinced!

David Evans, landlord of the Bull at Nettlebed. A larger than life character.

Loving the Swinging Sixties.

CHAPTER 4

Every Saturday, my brother, two stepbrothers and my mother and stepfather would go out to dinner or dinner dancing. Their greatest friend owned the gourmet hotel of the era, and here I was to discover at an early age the joys of oysters, green Chartreuse and angels on horseback, not to mention indulging in my first public cigarette and alcoholic beverage.

An average meal would have us accompanying the food with cigarettes between the five courses, expensive wines and ending up with liqueurs before we retired to the bar for some single malts. My stepfather told the boys that drams were the only permissible measurement! Welcome to Le Talbooth, the landmark eatery on the Essex-Suffolk border.

I vividly recall my mum stripping off to her underwear with her farmer friends, who would join us to swim under the river bridge that lit up the hotel. And there was the time when she misinterpreted frantic cries for appreciative cheers of encouragement as she attempted to leave the water by pulling herself out on the electric cables that lit the bridge and which could have electrocuted her.

I also recall that our host, Gerry Milsom, who was always ahead of the game, had bought one of the first stereophonic record players in production. We retired to his office (well after midnight to have him put on, at fullest volume, a recording of the 1812 overture, which must have been heard throughout the Suffolk and Essex borders!

Gerry Milsom OBE was one of East Anglia's most successful hoteliers and restaurateurs. He was the founder of Dedham's world-famous Le Talbooth restaurant, an idea conceived after stopping off at a half-timbered tearoom in Dedham in 1952. The visit was said to be at a low ebb in his life when he had just been demobilised from National Service in the Army; in an unlikely turn of events, the modest tea room was to transform his life.

As enchanted by the building as Constable before him, who captured it in his Dedham paintings, Gerry convinced his father to buy the 16th-century structure housing the tearooms – and Le Talbooth became not only the flagship of his business empire but one of Britain's best eateries.

With the help of his sister, Heather, and not put off by the restrictions of post-war rationing, Gerry built the business up and was rewarded with membership of the Relais et Chateaux group of luxury hotels and restaurants. His company, Milsom Hotels Ltd, grew to include two of Dedham's other upmarket venues – the Maison Talbooth hotel, which was bought in 1970, and the more modern Milsoms hotel bar and brasserie, which opened in 2008. The Pier restaurant in Harwich was also brought under his control in 1978.

Gerry's love affair with catering developed early on as he watched and learnt from his grandmother, a talented cook and teacher of domestic science. Born in 1930, he was educated at Epsom College and developed his culinary skills during National Service, where he spent the bulk of his time in the Catering Corps.

At Le Talbooth, the waitresses were pretty Swiss girls, the food outstanding and the host undoubtedly the best restaurateur I was ever likely to meet. So, at 21, I could hardly believe it when he asked me to be manageress at his 200-seat smorgasbord restaurant on the top floor of the leading private store in Colchester, with his best friend's fine wine store conveniently located just outside.

I was far too young and inexperienced to be running a restaurant, but for the 18 months it lasted, Gerry inspired me. In that short period of time, he taught me more than I could have learned in a lifetime of catering. When I worked for Gerry, I came to realise what a remarkable man he was. He always expected your best, and one tried so hard to provide it. He never missed anything; walking into a 200-cover restaurant, he would spot every customer and pick up on any small fault.

Married and divorced twice, Gerry adopted a Zulu boy in South Africa, where he owned a holiday home, and educated him at a leading South African public school. Sadly, Gerry died in Durban in 2005 after developing complications in a local hospital where he had been suffering from pneumonia for three weeks. I last saw Gerry at mummy's 90th birthday party at the Pier when he sailed down and gave a great speech. He and I sat and giggled over so many stories from the past.

Meanwhile, in Colchester, as Gerry's manageress, in the middle of the place, I had a glass office where I could survey my restaurant. I can see now the gleaming rows of dishes with the assorted smorgasbord in-front of a mirrored table, and then the amazing patisseries made by our superb European chef that were pushed around on golden trolleys, the waitresses colourfully attired with money belts under their aprons.

The opening day nearly proved my undoing and may count as one of the most terrifying days of my life. The owner of the store beneath the restaurant had requested that on our first day (which happened to be Wednesday), his staff should take advantage of early closing and enjoy a free meal. So, at 12.30, 200 hungry employees poured into the dining room, all expecting instant service, and all hell was let loose. Gerry's accountant, Bill Sykes, found himself wine waiter, and all those store staff ran happily amok.

After this followed one of Trude's classic clangers, one which my Colchester friends still dine out on. Following early closing day, we needed some way to bring in the diners, so we planned a businessmen's lunch and sent out 200 fliers. It was my habit at the time to post our takings in a money bag into the Barclays night deposit box. Whilst doing so, I would also deposit my post into a splendid letterbox with the word 'letters' writ large upon it in gold print outside the bank.

Thus, I posted in the 200 fliers. The next day, I was summoned to see the bank manager, who politely explained that the convenient gold post box actually belonged to the bank, not the postal service, and for the past few months, the night watchman had been re-posting my mail at the post office. The identity of Trudie, the postal menace, was finally revealed when he discovered a flyer to my gentleman's luncheon addressed to himself, the bank manager; hence, finally, the mystery was solved.

During the daytime, the cafe was a popular coffee stop, and I happily pursued friendships with various visiting beaux. It turned out that Gerry had a long-standing friend who came in one day with a friend, pointed a finger into my office, and said I'm going to marry that girl. And, you know what, he did!

Many years later, still enjoying a good lunch with Mummy and brothers Nevil, Mark and Francis.

My catering mentor, restaurateur Gerry Milsom, with his chefs at Le Talbooth.

The smorgasbord restaurant all ready to open in Colchester. Young boss Trudie is wearing the black cardigan.

The Offer

Every Thursday lunchtime, the Colne Restaurant of Williams and Griffin Ltd. will cater expressly for the business and professional men of Colchester, giving them the opportunity to meet freely without the restrictions incurred by belonging to any form of organisation.

The Service

Our intention is to present in comfortable surroundings a luncheon that has a special appeal for men, in traditional English style, or our celebrated continental cold table. The three course luncheon will be modestly priced at 10/6d.
There will be a bar available for pre-lunch drinks and a comprehensive list of wines for your enjoyment with your meal.
Although the Store closes at 1 p.m. on Thursdays, entry to the Colne Restaurant after 1 p.m. is via the main High Street entrance. The arcade affords entrance to the multi-storey Car Park immediately behind the Department Store.

The Conclusion

We feel that this idea can develop to our mutual advantage. We shall be pleased to hear any ideas which you may have to make it a greater success. Come next Thursday—We are confident that you will come again and again.
Reservations: Telephone Colchester 71212 ext. 62.

My flyer that ended up in the bank's letterbox. Note the invitation is for men only. Plus ca change...

CHAPTER 5

After the razzmatazz of Malta came the glamour of Gstaad. This is a place with a Swiss-German population and is a major ski resort that became very popular during the 1960s with the rich and famous of the world, many of whom sent their children to the renowned finishing school outside the town.

It was Aunty Vi who again found me a job in this winter wonderland. I was to accompany and cook for a French professor from Cambridge, who had bought a chalet a mile from the centre of Gstaad, which had once been a boy's boarding school. He was staying with his wife, two teenage sons, a daughter and a governess over the Christmas holidays. It was a wonderful job that only required me to cook breakfast, the occasional lunch and a 6 p.m. evening meal.

Thus, Trude had plenty of time to hit the slopes for the first time while befriending the world's rich and famous and dancing the nights away in Gstaad's only nightclub.

I spoke none of the local lingo, wallowed in my first duvet and discovered you could peel a week's supply of potatoes at the press of a mechanised button. How I relayed my orders to the butchers and patisserie bakers over the phone, I have no idea, and what turned up wasn't always exactly what I had intended. Why do hand gestures not work over a phone?!

The world's most famous finishing school, the Institut Alpin Videmanette, was down the road, which partially explained the presence of famous visiting parents and royalty who came and went to watch over (often out of necessity!) their adored daughters.

Throughout that winter, in my usual way, I befriended a local taxi driver who loaned me (very foolishly, if you know my driving) a huge American pink Plymouth car that I couldn't turn around or back! This was a beast of a car with a classic winged body and a six-litre engine. So it was that one morning while trying to negotiate one of the town's rare parking spaces, I heard a wonderful, deep and resonating Welsh voice so familiar from films. Unfortunately, there was more than a hint of anger in there as I had slipped the Plymouth in ahead of Richard Burton's Mini and pinched his slot!

Gstaad had two hotels, the huge imposing Palace Hotel overlooking the town and the Hotel Olden. It was to the tiny Hotel Olden that I gravitated towards because it was there that the rich and famous gathered. I had chosen a wonderful bar lady as my new best friend, so I was well looked after, and there was always a seat for me at the bar or in the restaurant.

One day, I would be chatting to the glitzy and stunning Elizabeth Taylor and her grumpy Welsh husband, whom I could listen to all day whilst feeling very glad I wasn't his wife. He was irascible and often not very nice to Elizabeth when out in public. On the other side of my table at dinner might be the beautifully elegant Princess Grace and her husband, Prince Rainier, who always remained quiet and polite. At the time, Lord Cholmondeley, one of the richest men in Britain, and the Aga Khan, known locally as Aly (also a competitive skier), lived in the town. Not far away was one of the world's most renowned violinists, Yehudi Menuhin; these were the circles I was fast becoming comfortable amongst.

In hindsight, I can see that I was being exploited by what I thought was an amorous Italian paparazzo who really just wanted to take me out for dinner in order to get a shot of the rich and famous with the camera he had hidden under the table. Gullible Me was the perfect front! Funnily enough, I met this naughty man a few years later on holiday in Venice with my mother and stepfather. Again, he took me out to dinner and then invited me back to his flat for a nightcap. (Do I never learn?) I went with some reservations, which were quickly realised when a few of his friends turned up to play poker. I was encouraged to join in, but I put down the cards when it was made too clear to me that this was going to be strip poker! In the best traditions, I made my excuses and left – but then had no idea how to find the hotel. I spent several hours bumbling around the many streets and bridges of Venice before getting back around dawn. I didn't dare ask for directions from anyone in case they thought I was on the game!

Back in Gstaad, life started to take a turn for the worse on 7th January 1966. Coming back from the nightclub, I had lost my key and couldn't get back into the chalet in the middle of the night, so I had to climb back in. Why, oh why, do I never get things quite right? I decided to climb silently up the balconies and get the governess to let me in. All was going well until I banged into the 15-year-old son's balcony, which made him call out for his dad! I'm afraid the professor misread the situation, believing that I was about to seduce his son – and ordered me to leave in the morning!

The following day dawned with a traumatic call from my family to tell me that my beloved father had sadly died in the night after a serious operation at the age of just 58. I was devastated. I have no idea how I made the journey home by train across to Geneva, from where I flew back into Southend in time for an extraordinary funeral. My brother Nevil and I sat behind the funeral coffin as it drove slowly past the 600 employees and shining rows of diggers with their buckets at half-mast lining the work's main driveway. It was a moment of pure sadness, and amazing to see so many of the employees weeping, too.

The Whitlock directors sent the following tribute to our family: 'The directors are conscious of the great debt which we all owe to Mr Whitlock for his unselfish and wholehearted devotion to the affairs of the company since 1924. Throughout a period of over 40 years, this devotion, coupled with his ability to organise and lead wisely and his skill, courage, determination and vision, brought the company great success and prosperity.

'All those who had the pleasure of knowing and working with him will miss his genial personality, his unfailing friendship and generous kindness and understanding. He endeared himself to all and was held in the highest esteem and greatest affection and respect.'

For myself, I feel Daddy has never left me, that he is always looking over me, trying to keep me out of trouble, while I hope

I occasionally make him proud.

After the funeral, I made another fraught journey back to Gstaad, where I discovered a very dear friend had arrived at The Olden to watch over me. This was Adrian, who was responsible for making the first plastic bags and used the money to buy a yacht. Now, he was writing a book called *Nits in My Beard* while following Ulysses' travels around European waters before the Mafia hijacked him off Corsica!

He was so kind, and as we entered the Hotel Olden, we were directed to the best table in the house. I should say here that Adrian was a dead ringer for the famous actor Peter Ustinov. Well, minutes later, the real Peter Ustinov appeared at our table – we had snitched his booking! So we all joined up, and a hilarious friendship developed. He was everything you would expect: full of fun and an extraordinary repertoire of entertaining stories.

By now, I had gathered my belongings from my previous employment as The Olden had kindly found me a room while I started looking for a job. I began at the top, going to Lord Cholmondeley – where I received a firm 'no', a young blond in the kitchen being deemed highly undiplomatic! And the Aga Khans had three professional chefs, so I was clearly outclassed there.

In due course, chalet Boomerang took me on for three weeks. They were an outgoing American family with five children. My main memory there is burying all the frozen food outside the kitchen door, deep in the snow, because the freezer was full. It was several days before I realised that a visiting fox or dog was peeing all over the spot – again, no one died!

Another hilarious moment came when the children wanted popcorn and, as so often, didn't get it quite right. I half-filled the largest pan with the popcorn and started cooking it... up it rose, and rose, until the entire kitchen – every nook and cranny – was liberally covered in popcorn!

I made my next contact through the job centre. She was married to the top banking man in Brazil, and they mostly lived on Avenue Foch in Paris. Her best friend was an agony aunt in a top magazine. My role was to be there when friends or family came and just to house-sit at other times - very much my kind of job, and there I stayed until the end of the season.

Madame was a wonderful cook and taught me so much about French and Brazilian cuisine, and was a pure joy. Oddly, though, I do recall her well-known guitarist son coming home once and sitting and firing pistol shots into a famous painting. Mostly, however, I lived in the basement, house-sitting.

Of course, I still had my taxi pal with his Plymouth, regularly filling it with ski instructors, followed by great dinner parties in the chalet. My social life, skiing and general hobnobbing continued happily; while the ski instructors would let me join their classes, we became friends, and life was good.

I made one final visit to Gstaad the following summer when my mum and stepfather John drove me there to see it in its summer greenery. After arriving at the Hotel Olden, I joined them outside their room before going down to dinner. Mummy announced she needed a wee and headed off to the room at the end of the corridor.

Unfortunately, she had walked into what was quite obviously neither her room nor the ladies' loo and disappeared into it, much to our amusement. On reappearing, she had been joined by one of the world's richest men, Baron Von Thyssen, who held open the door for her as mummy departed what must have been his private bathroom.

The Baron, with exquisite good manners, simply said: 'Good Evening, madame' and mummy replied: 'Thank you', with absolutely no idea of what she had just done!

Finally, one word of warning to poor little rich girls… the best-looking ski instructor taught the Elysee girls, and once a year, he would select one of the least attractive and intelligent students, take her out, and in due course propose – to the horror of the traumatised parents. The plan was simple: the instructor would visit the victim's home, rapidly receive a large pay-off from a distraught father and enjoy a good holiday before repeating the performance the following season.

The younger instructors always kept a chart of which girls they had bedded. I'm happy to say I only got one entry!

And that, dear reader, concludes my magnificent winter on the slopes.

Chalet Flora at Gstaad, where I scaled the balconies after a night out.

Living it large in Gstaad with Marcel, the taxi driver.

Ready for the piste: Note the carefully coiffed wig, curls pinned carefully in place underneath, ready for Apres Ski!

CHAPTER 6

It was the glorious Sixties, and freedom and the pill were upon us. As with so many of my generation, our ignorance was astounding: babies came out of your naval, and a French kiss was going to make you pregnant. Well, my experience in Chapter 1 had given me some education in the dealings of men and women, but I was still quite innocent despite my constant interest in the opposite sex.

I was not a sporty girl, but suddenly, I had a boyfriend who played hockey to England level, was a fast bowler for the Gents of Essex cricket team, golfed and played squash with some of the top players. My soon-to-be fiancé was James Neale, widely known as 'Champagne Jimmy' for his habit of loading a bottle of the bubbles in the back of his car for post-match consumption. We got married on 30th August 1969, shortly after my father's untimely death, fulfilling James' previously mentioned goal, 'I'm going to marry that girl', since it was he who spotted me in my office in Colchester at Gerry's restaurant.

We would go on to build a modernistic and very expensive house in an orchard owned by James' father, and while my new husband's law career began, I found myself on Saturdays driving players up to the prestigious Southgate hockey club, which he captained. The car, a smooth Jensen, accommodated our St Bernard in the back alongside casseroles filled with post-match curries and the ubiquitous champagne for when they won. On Sundays, I would be at Castle Park in Colchester watching cricket, where, in total boredom, I took up knitting, attempting unsuccessfully to stitch and purl the circumference of the boundary line, wasting acres of white wool that never made it right around. In the evenings, I would nip home to cook rounds of fried onions and hot dogs to accompany the after-game drinking.

Years later, in 1989, my step-niece, Sheila Nicholls, found a better way to deal with boredom at cricket matches. Aged 19, she did a naked streak at Lord's in an Ashes Test Match, performing cartwheels in front of a grinning Ian Botham. She found herself on the front page of every tabloid newspaper and went on to have a successful music career in America.

Meanwhile, our beautiful modern house, Fairlands, outside Colchester, won wide praise for its unusual design. I'm sure commuters on the Ipswich-Liverpool St line must have wondered what was going on as they made their commute to work and back. A newspaper report at the time described it as 'an uncompromising asymmetrical maverick of a building in which no two walls stand at right angles to each other and conventional standards of building, as epitomised by the rabbit-hutch school of architecture so common in modern estate bungalow development, has been cast aside.'

For a big house, there was not much conventional living space: three bedrooms, a living room, a dining room and a lovely kitchen. We also had a terrace going all around the house. There were problems when it came to fitting out the place because of the odd angles in all the rooms, so units had to be cut to fit, and the fact that the manufacturers switched from imperial to metric measurements in the middle of the project added wonderfully to the confusion.

The newspaper described it thus: 'An adventurous house, built to the precise requirements of a lively young couple who knew exactly what they wanted and were able to get it, Fairfields may not be to everyone's taste, but it is a welcome contrast to all that is drab in house design today.'

The builder was Ted Phillips, a legendary Ipswich Town footballer. Ted made over 250 appearances for the club between 1953-64 when Town rose from the old Third Division South to the top of the First Division under the guidance of World Cup-winning manager Alf Ramsey. Ted scored more than 150 goals, making him the third-highest scorer in the club's history. He also held the record for the most goals scored for the club in one season, 46, in the 1956–57 season, a season in which he was also joint-highest scorer in the old Third Division (now League One).

Ted was a wonderful rough diamond, a friend and a top bowler for the Gents of Essex and could make us cry with laughter about his illicit wanderings around the cricket team manager's house (he was a well-known titled landowner), deciding what he could do with the various items he came across, including brandy glasses, bidets, cigars and objects d'art.

Why is it that we are so fascinated by footballers? I well remember years later, in one of my favourite watering holes in Mauritius, wondering why, on arrival, every male room cleaner in the hotel would surround our bed in pure reverence. It turned out that Rio Ferdinand was the previous occupant.

On the hockey circuit of the 1960s, the Southgate club flourished. James practised on his pitch in the garden at Fairfields and continued on England training weekends. His teammates at the time read like a *Who's Who* of international hockey: Mike Corby, Tony Ekins, Bernie Cotton and David Whitaker progressing to distinguished playing careers with England and Great Britain. Roger Self, the coach, later managed the 1988 Olympic gold medal-winning side in Seoul, while Whitaker shared coaching responsibilities for the same team. James genuinely believed that his Southgate team laid the foundations for Britain's bronze medal at the Los Angeles Olympics and the 1988 gold.

I have many happy memories from this time, not least with Sue, one of my best friends over the years, especially at our skiing parties. Also, if you wanted to know the current fashions, you just needed to check us out, be it shiny white, red or gold long boots, the shortest minis or hottest hot pants, not to mention Carnaval Push-up Xtras (known as CPUs Xtra to be found in Carnaby Street) that raised your cleavage many inches. We had them all, and our evening wear surpassed even today's standards if it was possible.

Out on the slopes, we won a gold medal in Niederau, Italy, when the three wives formed a wonderful 'cow' to complete the obstacle course the instructors had laid out on carnival day. I was the back legs, Rosie was at the front, eyebrows were made from the skis' broom, while frankfurter sausages were hung as udders dangling below. Sue skillfully milked the cow all the way down the course. Fondue followed, and we ended the evening arm in arm with the boys while rendering their version of *Three Little Boys* very loudly'.

Another time, I managed to get things wrong again, having stupidly been left to make arrangements for a ski holiday to St Anton. Arriving at Luton airport, our four accompanying husbands were told that the plane had already left because I hadn't understood the European time difference. I won't repeat the verbal abuse that followed me! Actually, we luckily got the next plane out to Geneva and arrived before the other guests, even if a little too late to placate them!

Skiing, in the end, however, proved my undoing. Even after paying for private tuition, I discovered my skis wouldn't move because they had rusted up over the summer, and my old ski boot laces omitted a very unpleasant red drip behind my skis when I somehow managed to move at all. So it was tactfully suggested we girls abandon skiing and swap our skis for south-facing rooms, indoor swimming pools and flat roofs, where we watched to see who could make the biggest iced phallic symbols in the snow as we gently fried our bikini-clad bodies.

Away from the hockey pitch and the ski slopes, though, it sometimes seemed that James and I passed as ships in the night. Everyone thought our relationship was perfect, but in fact, we had very little in common and ended up separating when I was in my late 20s.

Before that, however, James' sister Carol and I were involved in a hilarious holiday on the high seas. Jimmy was training with England when she suggested I join them on our good friend's beautiful wooden boat for a week's break in Holland.

The only problem was that I get very seasick and the sea was rough. Also, I have no sailing skills, despite which I quickly found myself steering the boat. Oh well, I duly arrived in the harbour with my oil skins, a weekend bag and raring for adventure.

The other three quickly decided that my skills were best employed in the galley, having initially followed the wrong course, and I was sent below to cook them dinner. By now, I was not feeling well, and at this point, I lay on the skipper's bunk and felt very sick. No way could I be ill on this beautiful boat, but if I moved, I would be sick – and if I didn't, I'd wet myself because I was desperate for a pee. I was faced with two options. In the end, I quietly peed in my yellow waders – and what a wonderful relief – but every time a wave swelled up, the warm water in my waders swept up my legs and then dropped back down before the next wave!

In the morning, we arrived at Rotterdam old harbour at low tide, just as the early commuters were making their way to work above us. Carol and the two other crew members went off to buy breakfast and shower while I, still sitting with warm water in my boots and still feeling sick, said I would stay and clean up while they were away.

Very carefully, I pulled off my waders and got naked in the cabin... at which point the nausea gripped me again, and sickness seemed very close. I looked out of the porthole, where I spotted a bucket on the deck. Still starkers, I ran out and grabbed the bucket to run back into the cabin. Surely, someone could have told me the bucket was tied to the boat!

What a treat for the workers of Rotterdam to witness a naked lady wrestling with a stubborn bucket on a lovely wooden boat! I managed to make it back to the cabin minus the bucket, but the whole incident made me laugh so much that I felt almost human by the time the others got back. And so began one of the most fun holidays I have ever had.

I think I realised early on that marriage to dashing James was not going to work out, and this became very clear when, out of the blue, Carol suggested I join her on Lake Como to help look after her children and have a little fun, while her husband attended an accountants' meeting at the nearby Palace hotel. I needed little prompting, told James I was off and arrived to a beautiful mid-summer week on Lake Como.

One mid-summer night, we were joined by some of the world's top accountants and headed for a nightclub overlooking the lake. I can still recall every moment as I danced the night away with one of the gorgeous men in the group on the edge of the water where only the hiss of a passing halyard could be heard skimming across the water in the morning mist as a sailing boat passed.

The accompanying gentleman, from one of the leading American accountancy firms, became as carried away as I did, and a return to my hotel in the early hours soon followed. The ensuing letter that I received, I think, sums up those footloose days of the Sixties…

HEY TRUDE!

'Dearest Moon Maiden, you walked in and out of my consciousness so quickly, yet with such delicious impact that I am not yet sure who or what hit me! Midsummer's eve (less one week) will henceforth be on my mental calendar of events – though nothing could duplicate the mutuality of abandonment, singlemindedness of purpose, brightness of dawn, and thoroughness of coverage (Karma Sutra, indeed!). You mix a delightful moonlight cocktail – the taste lingers on, the intoxication permeates the mind and body and the hangover tingles and tempts. 'Til next midsummer moon. Jim'

I was put on the pill, the spirit of the Sixties roared on, as did I – and I think I left my first husband just in time. Twenty years later, James got himself into very serious trouble and ended up in an Australian prison.

In the 1980s, his life began to spiral out of control, leading to two jail sentences for fraud. He lost his legal practice in Colchester, running up gambling debts in Britain and Hong Kong, where Triad gangs brought him to account, and in 1999, his schizophrenic son Jonathan murdered his second wife, Rosie. His escape route from Hong Kong led to jail in Sydney.

In 2000, he agreed to ship a container of wine to Australia. However, the bottles included 'extras' that James claimed he believed to be quantities of Viagra. The Australian Customs took a close look and discovered A$14.8m-worth of Ecstasy tablets. With no bail in New South Wales for drug offences, he was sentenced to life imprisonment with a non-parole period of 21 years. I believe he is now back in the UK.

If James turned out to be a bit of a villain, I also came within touching distance of a few more infamous Essex residents over the years. We all think we are just normal, run-of-the-mill people, but then suddenly you ask if it can be normal to be on the periphery of four murders – probably not, but then I am an Essex girl!

It makes me wonder when I remember my good friend Patsy Bull, whose company I enjoyed. We shared a gardener together with her husband Wilfred, and I bought my first bureau from his antique shop in Coggeshall.

I had not expected, however, that Wilfred would go on to pretend that Patsy was a burglar in their shop and shoot her, her body shortly afterwards discovered by their son. It turned out that he had been having a long-term affair, and Patsy had threatened divorce, which would have decimated the business. For Wilfred, there was only one solution – and it cost Patsy her life and his freedom; he went on to serve a life sentence for murder.

Then, again in Coggeshall, there was my mother's doctor and family friend who died recently, still with no clue as to who had murdered his wife, Diane Jones, some years earlier.

In my young days, I learned to swim and enjoyed several Christmas parties at the Barn Restaurant in Braintree, where the owners, Bob Patience and his family, would later be viciously attacked by gunmen demanding access to their house safe. It cost Muriel Patience her life, while Bob and his daughter Beverley were severely injured.

The Bamber family, who were friends of my family, would also become victims in the terrible White House murders.

Their adopted son, Jeremy, would be found guilty of murdering his adoptive parents, sister and her twin sons after all five were found with gunshot wounds at their Georgian farmhouse in Tolleshunt D'Arcy in 1985. Despite serving a life sentence, Jeremy continues to protest his innocence.

Continuing the run of unusual and untimely deaths, not long after James and I split up, my stepbrother's cousin, who had a haemophiliac blood disease, died from AIDS after receiving blood transfusions that were later discovered to have killed many NHS patients; the compensation claims rumble on to this day.

But now, with James firmly in my rear-view mirror, a new chapter was about to open for me. I was about to become a responsible, happily married mum for a wonderful 18 years.

Marriage to James on 30th August 1969.

My leaving outfit, including favourite hat, after the wedding.

On the building site of our futuristic house outside Colchester. Ted Philips is on the right with our architect (left).

Inside Fairlands with Jojo, my first dalmatian.

Me and my enormous Saint Bernhard, Remy, in the garden at Fairlands.

Party animals: Me and James (with trademark bubbly) on the left on a skiing holiday with friends.

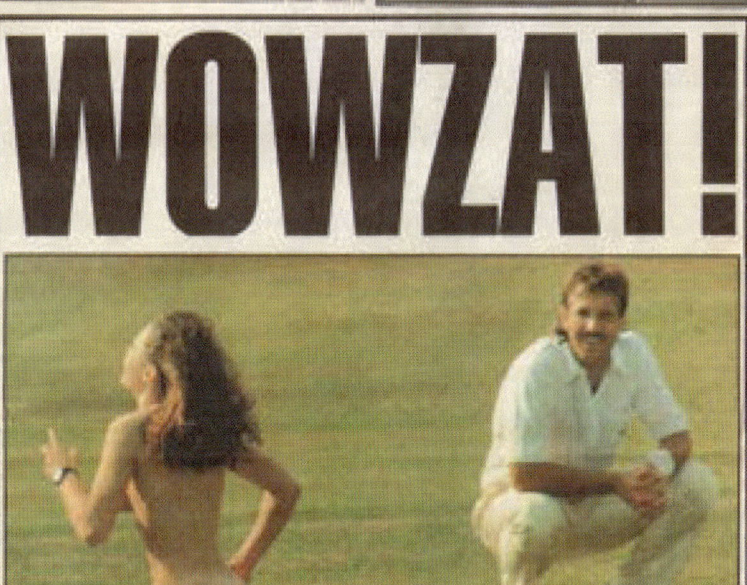

One way to overcome boredom at cricket. Niece Sheila Nicholls enlivens proceedings at Lord's.

Me and my great friend Sue, best friends since the '60s, on this occasion celebrating our joint 60th birthday.

Sue and I back in the '60s. The winning team with their skiing 'cow'.

CHAPTER 7

So the Swinging Sixties swung themselves out, the Suffolk coast called, and I found myself managing the Dolphin, a quaint seaside hotel in Thorpeness, while my seafaring master mariner sailed back from the southern seas to court me. Slowly, my country roots came back to me, the animals started arriving, and a confused P&O officer began to realise what he was taking on.

David and I met during one of his P&O leaves from the Southern Seas. It was when the Dolphin shut shop in the long winter evenings, we would sit chatting, and I fell hopelessly in love. I would drive my car along the coast road into Aldeburgh, singing at the top of my voice, 'I'm in love with a wonderful guy'.

The small but picturesque cottage that David had been left by a maiden aunt – whom he'd never even met (she simply had a picture of him on her piano shaking hands with the Duke of Edinburgh) – was about to receive an invasion as 'the Trude' moved in, complete with Penelope the cat, a herring gull with a broken wing, and of course Nimbus and Cumulus, my two young dalmatians.

I would skirt his little cottage near Aldeburgh Cinema and finally pluck up the courage to knock and request a coffee. The cottage had the bare essentials that weren't very warm, so we would hunker down in front of the fire where we mapped out our future. The one set of wicker furniture and a borrowed four-poster bed were all we seemed to need!

I persuaded David to forgo the Southern Seas and switch to driving the ferries between Felixstowe and Zeebrugge. So, in due course, we would put on our own event to match the Queen's and marry on the Silver Jubilee weekend, 4th June 1977; soon afterwards, a blushing bride could be spotted on honeymoon, sporting wellies, pulling tin cans behind her bicycle, heading for the boatyard and out across the Zuider Zee– discovering joyfully that she was pregnant. Slowly, David relaxed, feeling happy to be back at sea where he belonged. But the pregnant and seasick bride had other ideas.

Well, the Aldeburgh cottage was not a country estate, so at an otherwise tedious Aldeburgh cocktail party, I suggested to a couple who had downsized to a house overlooking Thorpeness (that was, in fact, much too big for them) that we should simply swap houses!

So, picture one very heavily pregnant young woman being driven in her jim-jams, with cat and dalmatians in the back of a Morris Minor, with David at the wheel on the way to exchange houses, passing over a mere £2,000 to the' swapees' to compensate for the lack of garage with the cottage. That's right – keep it simple, girl: bring the house name, swap the house, and bingo, we have a start on my country estate at Priors Oak – and David had hardly noticed I'd arrived pregnant!

What followed was the happiest day of my life. I had longed for Lucie to be born on 7th January – it was Nevil's birthday and the anniversary of Daddy's death – and. Sure enough, on that very date, my waters broke. I'd had a few problems in the pregnancy and had been advised to go straight to the hospital in Ipswich if there were any developments. I'm afraid I ignored the advice (along with all the prenatal classes that one is encouraged to attend) and spent the rest of the day with David, reading together *The New Childbirth* by Erna Wright. However, by the end of *The Generation Game*, I realised I had to go. We got there, and I was given sleeping pills, and David was sent home.

By 9 a.m. the following morning, I was being induced and waiting for David to turn up – which he duly did, bringing Nimbus and Cumulus with him, forgetting that dogs are not welcome in hospitals and that they would have to spend the rest of the day in the Morris Minor.

It was an overcast, misty day, and I lay on the fifth floor of the hospital, looking at the seagulls on a nearby rooftop. During each contraction, I tapped out the tune to 'The Sun Has Got His Hat On', changing the last line to 'and now the pains have gone away'. David, meanwhile, sat patiently by the bed, counting my four-minute contractions on his stopwatch from 11 a.m. to mid-afternoon, leaving the patient's bedside only to let the dogs out for a pee!

Next, I was wheeled into the delivery room, and I have to say it was all much easier than I'd been expecting. David had on his Dr Kildare white coat and mask, while our lovely young Irish midwife, Nurse Doyle, and the outwardly fierce but very kind Sister Nash made the whole event happy and relatively pain-free.

All that was needed was one big push. It took David to point out to Sister that blowing out my cheeks and going red in the face was achieving very little – but one last push and, oh my goodness, we had a beautiful little girl. How we gloated over our wonderfully tanned little baby, much more attractive than the pasty-faced creatures next door. But that rich colour turned out to be jaundice, and Lucie and I were confined to hospital for the next 48 hours. It broke my heart to see little Lucie lying in her incubator with a tiny net cap over her dark hair (later to fall out and return blonde), with huge cotton wool swabs over her eyes under a powerful lamp.

Of course, I wanted to get home as soon as possible, and with Sister Nash's encouragement, I tackled the paediatrician. She wanted me to stay, I wanted to go, and David sat silently, believing he was the referee. In the end, I threw a massive tantrum and howled and howled – and I got my way on the understanding that I must return the next day for blood tests, which I duly did, with huge hugs and kisses for Sister Nash and a V sign for the poor paediatrician, who was only trying to do her job.

So, now I was a mum, and just five months later, it emerged that I was pregnant again. This was not such a happy experience. Much of the pregnancy was spent in bed, with David and Lucie coming up to share meals with me in the bedroom. Finally, with bells ringing, an ambulance arrived, and we made our way back to Heath Road Hospital in Ipswich.

This time, I was not treated well – very badly, in fact. In the morning, I was told that I had miscarried and lost my son and further advised not to make a noise because there were women there having babies. For some reason, we called him Daniel, even though it was not a name that I particularly liked. Anyway, to help me get over the trauma, David took me to Madeira, where we stayed at the renowned Reeds Hotel. Gradually, I recovered, and life got back to normal as we returned to Priors Oak.

Here I must introduce, belatedly really, my wonderful Uncle Roy, who was Daddy's brother. He had fallen out with his parents over an affair with a lovely blue-rinsed dancer who was married at the time to a Roman Catholic. Roy's relationship lasted the course, and he and Jill finally married after her husband had died, divorce being heavily frowned upon in the Catholic church.

Our relationship actually began at my Christening as he was my godfather – I can't remember that, and he can't have realised what he was letting himself in for! Again, he toasted (a secretly pregnant) me at my 21st party, shortly before Daddy died, and Roy stepped in as my father figure, and a lifetime bond began.

When I married James, he sent us an enormous cheque to help with our new house; when I married David, he was there to give me away, helping with the house move and coming to clear the grounds at the start of our 10-acre garden project. Spanning the generations, Roy toasted Lucie at her Christening and later was a very calming influence in the two years before David's tragically early death.

We also comforted him through the sad time before his wife Jill's illness and death, and on a happier note, we had his pond enlarged into a trout lake and spent many happy hours fishing with him.

Every Thursday, my fabulous gardener Paul and I would spend the day with Uncle Roy, Paul keeping the garden going, and me doing the week's paperwork. One day, Uncle Roy looked a little worried and said he'd had a slight accident and dropped his Council Tax cheque into his urine bucket!

But he assured me that I shouldn't worry as he had dried it off down the bed, and I was handed one very smelly cheque to present to the council. When I got home, I rang the bank and explained to a teller what had happened. In a panicky voice, he assured me that he would post me a new chequebook immediately. Shame – I should have just sent the cheque to the council!

For the last ten years of his life (he would die in July 2002), his close companion was Snapper, his faithful Jack Russell (when he wasn't away courting every in-heat bitch in a 10-mile radius!). It was only when Snapper died that Roy took to his bed.

During his last three years, we drew ever closer, talking through his life from childhood onwards, how he left Whitlocks after the row with his parents, became an estate agent and pursued his love of country sports, not least helping to set up the first Game Fair. I listened to his private thoughts, and we had no secrets from each other. It was a very special time, with much joviality, laughter and some tears, but never a dull moment.

He touched the lives of so many ordinary people who passed through his life, however briefly, and was loved by so many of us. In one of his books, I found the following saying, which I think sums up my very dearest Uncle Roy:

'To the horses I've ridden; the quarry I've run;
To the hounds that I've followed, the waters I've fished;
To the acres I've covered with dog and gun;
Here's a tribute from one who has lived as he wished.'

Man and wife: Me and David married at Aldringham Church.

WINDSOR CASTLE

19th April, 1977

Dear Miss Neale,

    I am commanded by The Queen to thank you for your letter of 18th April and for your kind invitation to your wedding on 4th June.

    I fear Her Majesty is unable to accept your kind invitation. As I am sure you will appreciate, it would not be practicable for The Queen to accept all the invitations to weddings in her Silver Jubilee year and it is not possible to make exceptions.

    Her Majesty hopes nonetheless that it will be a memorable occasion.

Miss T.E. Neale.

Me and David invited the Queen to the wedding, but it was HM's Silver Jubilee, and she was otherwise engaged.

Getting a bird's-eye view of the 10 acres that were to become the garden at Priors Oak.

The same 10-acre view 45 years later. Credit: Richard Bloom.

Happy couple: Me and David on our wedding day.

Here's Lucie following 'the happiest day of my life'.

LUCIUS

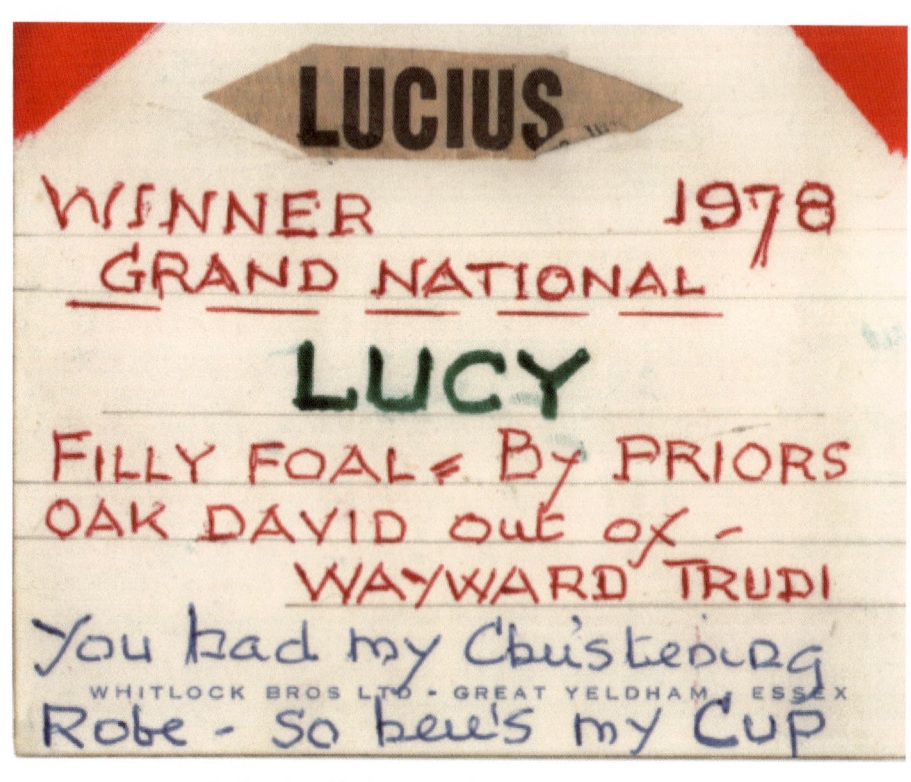

WINNER 1978
GRAND NATIONAL

LUCY

FILLY FOAL - By PRIORS
OAK DAVID out of -
WAYWARD TRUDI

You had my Christening
Robe - So here's my Cup

Confirmation of Lucie's pedigree from Uncle Roy after Trudie's last National winner.

With Uncle Roy showing off my fish from his trout lake.

CHAPTER 8

When David was away at sea, my mother would move in, and my beloved mentor Fred and I would set to work on a daily basis to help me achieve my rural dream at Priors Oak. Yes, David still managed to drag me down to the boat yards on his return, where we would yarn with the likes of the local characters Reuben and Jumbo while we helped to anti-foul the many waiting boats – but Priors Oak was my priority.

Here I must introduce Fred, someone who would become a huge influence in my life and a very good friend. Fred, who had taken early retirement from the Sizewell nuclear power station after an industrial accident looking after the boss there, found me bottling up, cleaning the Gents, cooking and serving in the bars at the Dolphin, and he had taken me under his wing, helping me out of all sorts of scrapes as well as making life a lot easier for me by mucking in at the pub.

The chef walked out a week before Christmas, and he simply came in every day to help me, carving the ham for Christmas breakfast, the turkey for dinner and helping with the buffet in the evening – with a change of jacket and bow tie for each event)

Fred was a local man of many talents. His mother, the local Mrs Fixit, had brought him up to collect animal hair off hardwire fences to cure warts, fill baths with gin to deal with unwanted pregnancies, do the milk rounds, and keep livestock (where castrating was simply done with a quick bite of the teeth.)

He spent a happy war guarding Box Hill in Surrey and Buckingham Palace. And, as a young man, he was lucky enough to run after the Zeppeplin that crash-landed at Theberton and collect pieces to sell as paperweights and souvenirs to the locals. (Later, my daughter Lucie would do a school project on the event, and Fred reinvented the exact journey for us, revealing that a pair of lady's high heels were discovered, sparking the rumour that a woman must have been aboard. In fact, it emerged the shoes belonged to the female half of a courting couple racing away from the crash).

Fred, who also became gentleman's gentleman to the boss of Cunard, taught me all I know about Suffolk, using phrases like' if they come the old acid over you' and words like 'ranny' for a mouse as well as all the local weather jargon. I could ramble happily on about Fred, who was to become my best friend, start my garden and be there for every family event – Lucie's Christening, granny's surprise 70th birthday party, David's 40th, and so much more – helping to make every occasion go well until he sadly died in 2000 in his nineties.

He planted the magnificent oak tree that perfectly describes Priors Oak; he was there the night we moved in (me in pyjamas and nine months' pregnant). There were just so many happy times that I spent with this man – so much laughter and happiness and so much back-breaking work!

Because now, at Priors Oak, life was taking on a new pace, and the promise of sheep, donkeys, tortoises, ponds, bogs, and ducks was all on Fred's agenda for me. Perhaps I could sink an old basin and make a pond? No, no, no came Fred's response, and he persuaded me, in David's absence, to sink an old fibreglass dinghy that he never used, surround it with paving stones and plantings and, believe it or not, it took David quite a few days to discover his hidden dinghy!

Then the serious work started, with Fred making me dig five-foot deep ponds, clearing the brambles, gorse and rough stuff. Then there were the identical twin farmers who helped with all farming chores, stood me between them and showed me how to broadcast grass seed by hand with a fiddle. I did my first three acres, which grew and cropped beautifully – and then the rain came, my beautiful rows of hay stooks would turn to mush, and my hay-making days were over!

Wasting no time, we scrumped mallard eggs from the mere for my new pond, searched out donkey sales, and the next sheep sales for when David was on leave. Ben, a young donkey from Norfolk, was the first to arrive and how appropriate that he was named after Suffolk coast's Benjamin Britten, who was to live happily, if stubbornly, with us for 36 years.

The next excitement was making up Fred to look like our head herdsman and attend a Suffolk sheep dispersal sale. My heart pounded when, at the end of the catalogue, the last elderly in-lamb ewes were to be auctioned. There, in black and white, I read 'Sire of the Great Yeldham Most Amazing' – so a genuine descendant of my great grandfather's flock. I just had to have her and, to this day, the ear tag for old Sal (as I called her after my so-close relationship with Nevil's daughter Sal in Australia) has been sown into Sal's and Lucie's wedding dresses, accompanied Lucie's friend Chloe to New Zealand to help set her romance on a firm footing, and never missed an important family event. Today, it sits poised in my jewel box at the ready for its next outing.

Chloe was three years older than Lucie, but they became fast friends at an early age. They would play together unwatched over the next five years of play, with much laughter and mischief. I very much doubt two children had more freedom or fewer rules than Lucie and Chloe, and the fun seldom stopped. Animals abounded, from hamsters, guinea pigs, the odd hedgehog, and tame rabbits to the wild ones that they bred. A raised swimming pool added to the entertainment; apparently, I was an unconcerned mother.

After a while, I decided they needed to know what life could be like and to know what to do if needed. It was David's belief that they should know how to change a damper plate on a sailing boat in Cornwall in mid-November; Mum, on the other hand, thought they should know how to enjoy a cream tea in full regalia at London's Cafe Royal and, aged 10, share a suite at the Ritz! The sight of them lifting the silver dome covers to reveal their treats and then gawping unashamedly at shower heads bigger than the loo seats was just hilarious.

Chloe never let me down! A trip to the Lloyd-Webber show of the time was notable for the sight of me dragging her barefooted across London in case she fell over inappropriately high heels. And I can see her now in the Ritz being asked what she would like off the menu as ice cream and strawberries, and several courses just disappeared.

Then, at half term, we were off to the Marine Palace Hotel on the Devon coast. It was populated by nice visiting families in their best tweed and plaid skirts and long socks, and then I spotted a 13-year-old Chloe arriving in the dining room in full make-up (with Lucie in tow, all made up, too) with an outfit to match, while dancing a tango between the tables of astonished diners. I leant across to David with a very heavy aside please to say nothing or we'll embarrass Chloe.

To my absolute delight, I learned years later that Chloe was taking her daughter Daisy up to London to celebrate her 18th birthday at the Ritz. A fine tradition!

Meanwhile, Fred insisted that a young Lucie needed a Wendy house. So, neatly killing two birds with one stone, we kept David happy by bringing the sea to the garden and delighted Lucie with our Pansy. This came to us via a retiring Scottish electrician, who planned to sail up to Scotland on his sailing boat Pansy to live out his retirement. It was an ancient sailing boat with a wonderful wooden sash-windowed boathouse held up by wooden pegs, complete with steerage and engine room equipment.

Sadly, the journey was to prove too much for Pansy and its owner Mr McDonald, so he decided to replace it with a modern-day fibreglass boat. With much elbow grease and the loan of a tractor, Pansy arrived (goodness knows how we did it) on the Priors Oak Rockery – and Lucie undoubtedly had the best Wendy House on the east coast.

Yes, Fred and I had done it, and all around us, sheep were lambing, the ponds were filling with hatched mallards, Ben would be grazing happily with a variety of friends such as the rams, a retired Welsh Mountain pony or Welly, the bad-tempered Shetland. Exotic chickens were roaming the grounds; tortoises started arriving, as did cats, dogs, guinea pigs, and Fiver, a giant lop.

The Suffolk Show was on one year, and the poultry shed drew me in to discover a beautiful silver cockerel who serenaded us. I wanted him. The elderly owner agreed on a price, and soon, my six Rhode Island Reds had their own male. We left him to roam Priors Oak with the girls, but, alas, there was no sign of him at lock-up time.

However, at dawn, the crowing would begin, but it was only after the third night that a rather disgruntled neighbour complained, and we were able to find him. It transpired that Silvester had never before left his fancy cage, seen grass or water. We found him forlornly standing on the island in the middle of our pond: wet, soggy and confused. Back in the house, he revelled in a hair wash and blow dry with my hairdryer. From then on, he crowed happily all night – and was very much on our neighbour's death row list.

So what were we going to do with my beautiful Silvester? At the time, Lucie was a day pupil at Brandeston Hall, junior school to Framlingham College, and one day, when I collected her, I asked Arbon, the long-standing gardener, if he kept chickens. Yes, of course, and he would take Silvester. He would put him in a box in the school shed, and feeling a little nervous, I did as requested.

I dropped off Silvester on a Friday evening. On the Monday, Lucie told me: 'Oh dear mummy, Silvester was outside the headmaster's house where he crowed all night!' Here's a tip –

you don't let a cockerel out in your daughter's private school adjacent to the headmaster's bedroom! I went looking for a completely unconcerned Arbon, who said all the ducks were gay, so he had just let Silvester loose on the grounds, confident that he could cause no harm.

The Christmas carol service loomed, and we all queued up to shake hands with the head. Very firmly, he held my hand and looked me in the eyes, wishing me a Happy Christmas and a very peaceful New Year! The headmaster's wife later penned Silvester in with some ladies, but I'm afraid he did eventually disappear.

Other animal guests included tame Indian Runner ducks gifted by David's fellow seaman and chief stevedore friend from the Zeebrugge docks, a man who, he said, often kept his sanity going. Cor De Zoette and his wife became great friends of ours, bringing their family over at least three times a year, while his input into the garden with his woodworking skills was never-ending.

Animal life never went completely to order at Priors Oak – and everyone remembers the years of Due the Dutch Indian Runner. On her incubated birth, she quickly bonded with Dougal, my long-haired Pointer, and never left his side, pleading to be trodden on most of the time. Dougal was a saint and just accepted this strange partnership.

However, each year, Due had a phantom pregnancy and would go into decline, so in desperation, I stuck a chicken's egg under him by his small pond – and, as a result, Archbishop Desmond Tutu arrived! All proved well until the baby tried to swim and sank – after which he dutifully watched the pond from the safety of the edge.

Eventually, Desmond grew into a cockerel intent on raping poor Due! I'm afraid the Archbishop had to be posted elsewhere to service my neighbour's flock.

Around this time, I was looking for wood to make another shelf for my books. David obliged, and in due course, I was told a gentleman had arrived with the wood, but he needed some help. I had not expected a low loader outside the house loaded with an entire planed oak tree felled in the 1985 gales! Cor used these planks throughout the garden for years to come, as decking around the chalet, lovers' seats, arched gateways, bookshelves, and so much more.

In 2005, I did my final big buy and built a brick wall down the garden with enough Aldeburgh Reds (local clay brick to build five bungalows. I ran out of money for the Maggie Hamlin gates, so Cor just brought his old front door down and stuck it in the wall where it resides happily today.

Cor and his family were a regular and feature in our lives for a good many years; there was no job too extreme for Cor and Alan, our then gardener. Alan, alongside Cath, his wife, became our good and close friends. He was a superb gardener, and David and I spent happy hours with them both, constructing things for the garden or lambing with Fred, while they would also house-sit for us on our annual holidays. Alan, ever the practical joker, would tie runner beans on my plants, find the longest nettle, or discover my aged old Sal had produced quads aged 15.

HEY TRUDE!

At the end of Alan's time, Paul came on the scene in the garden (and is still with me now), as well as the lovely board-treading Rufus, who joined us for 10 happy years, helping in my wildlife garden where he learnt his lines, set 100 rat traps that only ever caught three mice (but planted three plastic rats that can still be found in unexpected places in the garden!), made us laugh and was always prepared to give Paul a hand on open days and whenever needed generally.

His legacy is Mavis, a polystyrene lady first spotted in a Halifax Building Society. Mavis is now happily ensconced in our carport conversion aptly named The Greasy Spoon Tearoom, complete with black plaits, fearsome make-up, painted nails and fishnet stocking. A stuffed cat sits on her lap, a stuffed Retriever at her feet, and a glass of gin is at hand. Mavis doubles as a very useful security guard, regularly scaring the pants off unsuspecting visitors!

Ru had a happy life with his partner Jill, and it was my privilege to give the eulogy at his funeral - even though he did steal the heart of my Labrador dog Mango! Remembering Mango, I recall a day when Lucie, myself and David spent the day on Richard Branson's Necker Island. We were staying on one of the nearby British Virgin Isles and decided to sail across to Necker for a picnic. On arrival, another Mango, Richard's dog, stole all our picnic and iced tea!

After Ru sadly died, his old friend Pete came to take his place as Mr Fixit and wildlife helper. We had a remembrance service for Ru at Kesgrave Hall, where I gave a eulogy, which was interrupted in a rather amusing (very Ru) way.

I was sitting well-placed at the front next to my farming friend Mike (then 80). I stood to start reading, and immediately, Mike's mobile started to ring. In a wonderful moment, he answered it and announced to everyone quite loudly that it was Ru calling!

The mobile kept on ringing happily throughout my eulogy and went on as everyone in the audience did their best to get hold of Mike's phone. A wonderful last laugh with Ru!

While at Priors Oak, David went into partnership with a friend, Tony Graham Enoch, and they created some 36 popular kitchen retail shops, most of which had restaurants attached. The company was Spoils, which they founded in 1975, soon turning over £35 million a year in stores piled high with plates and cups and everything you could need in the kitchen. At the start, we had guaranteed it with the deeds of our house and in those early days, we spent much of our time between Aldeburgh and the potteries in Stoke-on-Trent, searching for seconds and bringing them back to David's friend Tony's house where we stored them.

However, over the years, it fell victim to increased competition and reduced profit margins. Spoils was forced into receivership in 2005, by which time David had passed away. Throughout the Spoils period, he remained on the ferries, mainly for the seafaring companionship and the belief that you always kept a safe job behind you.

Before that, however, came the traumatic events of 6th March 1987, a night I shall never forget. This was when P&O's Herald of Free Enterprise went down when the bow doors were left open, and tragically, 193 lives were lost.

HEY TRUDE!

Unbeknown to me, David was on the sister ship that night, so when I turned on my radio to hear the alarming news, I believed for several minutes that it was David's ship, and I just knew that he would have been among the last to leave a sinking ship I honestly thought I had lost him.

David personally knew the crews, many of whom were friends, and some of the survivors never came to terms with what happened; David himself suffered for a long time to come. In the end, he and a close engineer friend started a software company dealing with the stability of large shipping, which still flourishes under another name to this day.

David firmly believed the Herald was an accident waiting to happen, and whenever he was sent up to Newcastle for the annual drydock, he always sent in reams of safety suggestions that the company felt uncomfortable about, which was probably the reason he never made captain as P&O must have feared that he would never set sail!

He was a man of high principles and scrupulous honesty - just a wonderful guy. He wanted to show Lucie and me the secret hideaways of the world that he had discovered in his cruise ship days. A man who lived for his love of maps, off-road exploring, snorkelling, diving and living off the land. If hunger took us, we climbed mango trees; thirst was solved up a coconut palm! Or maybe a freshly cut raw sea urchin.

Two weeks a year saw us going off around the world, seeking out his favourite haunts around the World. Off-road, we might suddenly turn up at a still fully working leper colony or, in the Caribbean, hit roads closed off because of robbers – nothing phased him, and somehow, it was easy to trust in him and his judgement. From Australia, walking the hills in Hong Kong, playing with elephants in Thailand, Africa and Sri Lanka, while sailing the waterways in the British Virgin Isles – we saw it all.

Maybe David's family were responsible. His great-grandfather left school at 13 to become a house boy, chauffeur and railway mechanic and eventually a university graduate. From a lowly upbringing, Harry, David's father, would become a professor who, together with six other friends, became a world-leading spectroscopist, focusing on the fusion of plastics, travelling around the globe, including behind the Iron Curtain, to lecture.

His wife Jennifer, David's mother, was a war wife and encouraged by the government to breed – which she did, producing seven children, albeit somewhat reluctantly! However, of the seven, only Nancy still survives. Sadly, Nancy was wheelchair-bound at 16, with a life expectancy of under 30. That was proved completely wrong, and this year, aged 70, Nancy's paintings have appeared in the Tate Modern gallery, and she has won overseas awards for short films that she has created.

Jennifer was a true eccentric, expelled from schools and university, preferring to focus on helping the mentally handicapped. A founder resident of the first garden city (Welwyn), her eccentricities were boundless, be it regularly walking a tortoise once around the garden – always in the same direction and always allowed to eat one dog turd – or providing her family with the exact same diet weekly: three lettuce leaves, half a turnip, bottled vegetables and fruit, probably the most unappetising food you've ever set eyes on. But for all her many eccentricities, she established a huge legacy working with local mentally handicapped ladies.

Meanwhile, in his late forties, David began to feel unwell and was later diagnosed with Spinal Muscular Atrophy. For the next three years, he was to prove the most remarkable and steadfast husband, never complaining, always making the best of things, and he began collecting first editions of old books. He took to going out in search of first editions and reading all the old classics.

Wheelchair-bound for a long time and on a breathing machine (which we plugged into the cigar lighter in the car like an elephant's trunk!), Papworth Hospital lent us massive equipment so he could live out his life at Priors Oak. Carers came to help all day, and life was sometimes very hard, but never did David complain, lose his sense of humour or his determination to survive; he just wanted to be with us. I can't profess to being a natural carer or very good at it, but we were immeasurably happy all the same. How often I tipped the electric chair out of the boot, and couldn't find the hole to give it a wipe while on the hoist (still struggling with my facts of life!).

Eventually, to the quiet strains of Judith Durham on his gramophone and 'There Will Never Be Another You', he quietly gave in to death, aged just 49. The funeral was attended by masses of people, and the church played out *Johnathan Livingston Seagull* by Neil Diamond and *I Must Go Down to the Seas Again* by John Mansfield was read.

At last, David could run the waves again and sail away, and Lucie and I had lost a truly remarkable man.

After her dad's tragic death, Lucie decided a break was in order before university and, wondering what to do, I first sent her on a typing and shorthand course, then a cordon bleu course (her cooking skills were nil!) and finally on a Dragoman Land Rover trip across Africa, ending up in South Africa.

She had befriended a South African waitress and, through her, met and began seeing Tyrone Pascoe from East London in the Eastern Cape Province of South Africa. At the end of her Dragoman trip, she ended up in Tyrone's East London home and decided that now a degree was necessary. She took her degree, was awarded a scholarship and settled into life with Tyrone and his family. They returned briefly to live in Trowse, outside Norwich, but Tyrone's roots and family were in South Africa, and they settled there in due course.

In 2003, all his friends and family arrived to celebrate their marriage in Aldeburgh Church. This is when you realise what happens at a marriage when there is no guiding father figure at hand. Lucie and I simply did it all!

With his eight best men from his college class, they stood outside the pub with top hats pulled down to their noses and freezer ties on their shirts as cufflinks were not on the agenda – They certainly gave me some very odd looks when I'd asked previously for their inside leg measurements for the morning suits!

As to the wedding, no expense was spared, from a horse and cart to the church and back to Priors Oak, an afternoon of jazz in the garden with a free ice cream van arriving mid-afternoon, to a double hog roast in the evening, and finally, an Irish band that shook the rafters, we had it all, and it lasted several days (the cost best not mentioned!).

Lucie has made her home in South Africa and produced my two wonderful grandchildren, Mila and Oli. Mila is a beautiful ballet dancer and choreographer, while Oli, my magical grandson who, at 13, was sponsored for his surfing prowess, continues to thrive at the sport. I have a family that I am so proud of and whose manners and upbringing is, as anyone will tell you, exemplary. David would have been so proud.

Fred, modelling Trudie's glasses.

Farmer Trudie with quad lambs, they appeared in the paper when they were miraculously born to Old Sal at age 15.

Chloe, Aussie Niece Sally, and Lucie, all recipients of 'Old Sal' the sheep's lucky ear tag

Pansy, the best Wendy house on the east coast.

Cor installing his front door in the newly built garden wall.

Mango, Ru and Paul in the garden.

Pete hard at work coppicing.

The indispensable Joy who quietly potters, magically transforming corners of the Priors Oak garden.

Oz holiday: Me, Lucie and niece Sally, 1987.

On the road in Thailand.

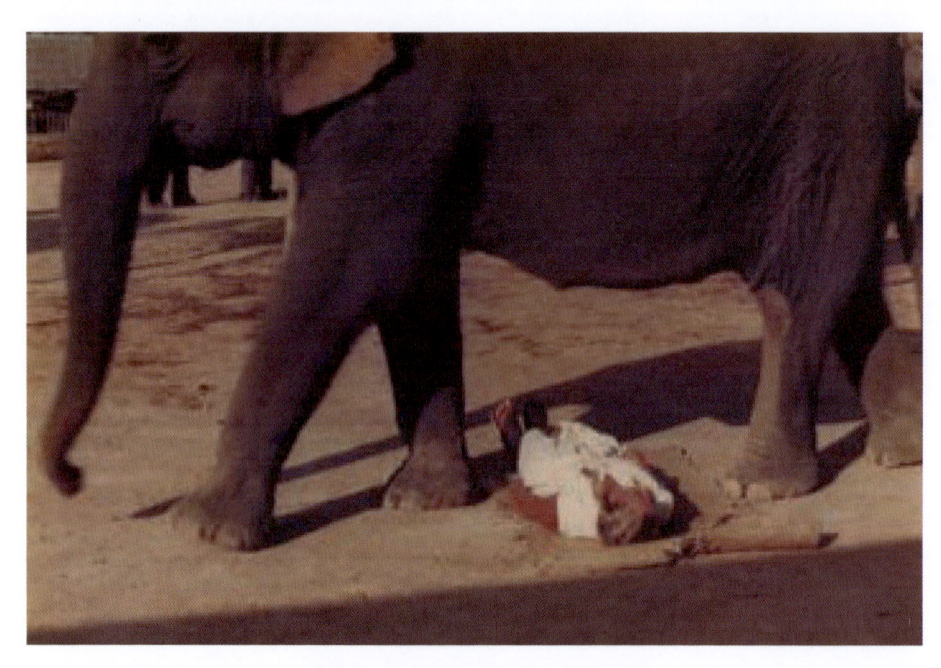

It has to be Trudie under there in Bangkok.

Me with my 'Willis sisters', Pat (right) and Nancy.

Happy day: Lucie and Tyrone pose for photographs in the garden railway carriage.

It seemed that I may have got my inside leg measurements wrong, as Tyrone's dad found out!

Four family generations with granny (my mum), on the left, me, Mila, Lucie and Oli.

CHAPTER 9

Suddenly, I was a wealthy 50-year-old widow with a string of unsuitable suiters. What to do? My friends took it upon themselves to find me a safety net and rescue me quickly. Out of the blue, a girlfriend said she was arranging a blind date for me. She'd found a retired Royal Navy commander who must surely be in with a chance given that he drank pretty heavily, chain-smoked and played golf all day; he was 10 years my senior but had his own cottage up the road and occasionally made mildly inappropriate remarks – but would be no bother.

The date was set for the dinner party – and Roger arrived in my life.

Strangely, this larger-than-life, very unpredictable man proved to be just the safety net I needed: he only appeared when the pink gins had run out at the 19th hole; he dropped around for me to cook a nice meal and would take me twice weekly for happy hour at the pub for boozy, happy sessions with friends. In the ensuing years, I took the commander to some of the best hostelries in the country and holidayed with him for years in my beloved Mauritius, all the while waiting for the next disastrous comment, something which was never far away.

For example, some motorcyclists came into the bar, and he asked them to remove their fancy dress. Another time, a lady popped in to order six orange juices from the bar, and he said it shouldn't be allowed in a pub. When she explained the drinks were for her several children, he suggested her husband must be hung like a baboon, one of his catchphrases!

When my mother was at home, she and Roger would glare daily at each other over the golf and rugby on the box like an old married couple, seeing who could get rid of the other first, but they never actually did.

One day, Roger and Mummy had a particularly heated disagreement, resulting in Roger storming out of the house in a huff back to the sanctuary of his cottage. Fearing she may have caused trouble for me, Mummy decided to write to Roger to apologise. However, my Mother was still pretty angry so before penning a rushed apology, she offloaded her true feelings on paper in a journal-style rant in which she wrote down, in rather colourful language, exactly what she thought of Roger, having let off steam, she proceeded to draft out her actual letter of apology. Rushing so as not to miss the post, she stuffed her apology in an envelope and sped off to the post box so as not to miss the last collection. Imagine her horror later to find her neatly written final version of the apology still sitting on the table – Yes – Mummy had accidentally sent Roger her scribbled draft, complete with her therapeutic 'Roger bashing' rant on the reverse! It seems Trude was not the only one in the family who didn't always get things quite right!

After 10 years, he developed Dupuytren's contracture in his golfing fingers and managed to creep into my house to get the TLC he craved. Once ensconced, he could be found, fag and gin in hand beside a large evergreen, demanding to know when I was going to concrete the bloody lot.

There was no way that was going to happen. David, Fred, Cor, Alan and Cath, Rufus and Paul had invested too much effort in 10-acre Priors Oak for that to happen. I like to think of our garden here as a series of rooms and hope that the odd surprise will appear around the corner. To me, it's been like painting a picture with a forever-changing landscape. The garden usually dictates to me, rather than the other way round.

It became only natural for me to share what we have, and we instigated the Open Days, which have proved popular with visitors as well as raising over several years more than £60,000 for a wide range of local and national charities, something I'm very proud of, especially as most of the money has come from donations rather than a fixed entrance fee.

In the garden, we've set up lots of surprises and unexpected treats: visitors might bump into donkeys or sheep; real and sculpted tortoises; nesting boxes for birds and bats, chickens, frogs, and, of course, our fairy area leading up to the decorated caravan, which declares 'adults may enter if accompanied by a responsible child'!

I make no apology for admitting that the gardens are my obsession. It's why we're constantly looking at ways to keep them in good condition as well as developing them. Within, we have the chalet, a good spot to observe the wildlife, but also a bit of a shrine to my family – the Mills and the Whitlocks – with some amazing relics from their time. Also, in 1990, we took delivery of two railway carriages, in which you can now catch up on wildlife facts, while on open days, there is always a cup of tea available in the 'Greasy Spoon'.

Through drinking mates, I met Josef Waldrak, a former top London interior designer and connoisseur extraordinaire of fabrics and design, and he first made his remarkable presence felt when he turned my carport into the Greasy Spoon restaurant, which can seat 40 tea-taking visitors. This amazing indoor/outdoor room can be opened to the elements in winter and summer. It is filled with South African and Sri Lanka colour, love and, above all, fun – once seen, never forgotten!

Next, Josef offered to undertake the renovations to Tresco, the neighbouring home, bought by me as a home from home for my South African visitors and a holiday let, as required. Josef's colour schemes have brought the accommodation to life, with large dog-proof gardens and an area to lounge in the sun. Just stepping into Tresco, you are hooked by colour, style and a feeling of pure peace and immediate love for the house; my visitors never want to leave.

So now I look over my 10 acres, two houses, railway carriages, family museum and wealth of habitats and animals, and it just oozes love and tranquillity within my boundaries. I would not be alone in saying it has peace and immediate love that just overcomes you.

My house is now no longer visible under its foliage, and every morning, I wake up smiling and offer a prayer of pure thanks at the end of the day. With nearly 80 years behind me, I look happily over the estate, and it has been my pleasure to be its custodian for the past 45 years. And here I must pay tribute to Paul, my long-time friend and gardener for the last 20 years, who has contributed so much to what we have so lovingly achieved together.

Built on poor sandy soil, my garden would never have flourished were it not for the significant impression made on me by the rubbish heap that Daddy's gardeners established at Gt Yeldham, where, aged six or seven, I would sneak to watch the rats eating and cleaning their whiskers. I always admired these much-maligned creatures until one of our cats dumped one on my bed!

Anyway, this gave me the idea to start our own at Priors Oak, started by the manure from the donkeys, sheep and chickens. All the scraps were kept from the kitchen and added once a week while we supplemented it all with the magic ingredient: Russian comfrey (which soon spread, unwanted, into every corner of the garden). We topped it off with straw bedding and a liberal scattering of calcified seaweed from Cornwall, a terrific compost accelerant. Early success was measured in the prizes from the Knodishall Flower Show, where my vegetable box beat off the famous perennial winner, Spud Murphy.

As the garden grew and we bought more land, so too did the heap. We didn't have bonfires because the ground was so dry, so all garden weeds, old wood, spent vegetables, and grass mowings went into the ever-expanding compost. This is how I explain to visitors why my buddleia competes in size with the cedar trees or provide a reason for our 12ft high fennel.

HEY TRUDE!

Early every spring, we drive the tractor over the heap and flatten it out while I scatter any old seeds I have to hand – wildflower mix, gourds and nasturtiums – to add a little extra colour. So, for those of you who prefer your brown bins stuffed with garden waste in neat rows along the street, I say save some money and enjoy a touch of countryside magic!

It was summed up for me one day when a wheelchair-bound lady visitor carefully stood up and gave me a huge hug, exclaiming that there was more love, laughter and peace in my garden than anywhere else she'd been. I thought that was wonderful.

Was all this really not to my friend Roger's taste? I think he was just being provocative when he urged me to order in the cement mixer. Well, that was his way – along with his habit of walking out on me. Once, he did this just before my birthday, leaving me with an expensive air ticket to Mauritius to fill.

I insisted that a male escort must join me, Lucie and my long-suffering son-in-law on this super holiday. Regulars at the pub all made helpful suggestions, and, in due course, an old purser friend of David's was found, and Trude was back on form. The happily broke purser, living on a Dutch barge outside Heathrow, fancied a free ride – who wouldn't? I believe everyone should do this once in a lifetime!

I duly arrived at the airport with my entourage of luggage to be met by my new companion with his tiny backpack. I should add that my publican friend turned up in his taxi to take me to the airport, arriving in Bermuda shorts and sunhat in case I'd changed my mind and he could join the party!

On arrival, I had completely forgotten that I had requested a late honeymoon upgrade (never one to miss a bargain!) for Roger and me. So the ex-purser and I met the manager who, with great pride, took us up to the newly decorated honeymoon suite! There, the white four-poster was strewn with flowers, as was the sunken jacuzzi, while champagne and canapés were everywhere. We lay on the bed and howled with laughter. For the next two weeks, my wonderful purser settled me on the beach, danced with me and made me laugh while my bemused son-in-law looked helplessly on.

Another time, I was enjoying a South African holiday with Lucie and her family in Cape Town and East London when former president Nelson Mandela's health began to weaken. Immediately, the authorities went into overdrive, rapidly preparing the great man's home village so dignitaries from around the world could safely fly in to pay their respects when the time came. The logistics were huge, and time was running short.

Meanwhile, on the other side of the world, I was receiving news that the waters were rising around Roger's cottage in Snape, and he was preparing for a flood, trying to move furniture while watching the deteriorating weather conditions. At the same time, at Priors Oak, a worried Paul was trying to find barriers to prevent damage to the gardens.

I was due to fly out of South Africa the following day, and on waking in the early hours, I was expecting to see a post on Facebook from the River Alde, updating the flood situation back home. Instead, I saw that Mandela had died.

HEY TRUDE!

The day ahead proved to be memorable, and travelling through Johannesburg at that time was an experience not to be missed. When I arrived at East London's little airport, I was transported into a lounge where members of the ruling ANC party were gathering to fly to Jo'burg for the funeral.

I felt very out of place, sitting quietly at the back while the VIPs paraded in beautiful hand-made ceremonial robes, the colours simply radiating, but the sadness was overwhelming. As the local leader received each of them, I knew what a mammoth moment in history I was witnessing.

Back in Snape, Roger was watching the waters swirl around the cottage and finally enter his back door; the view now revealed a swollen road onto flooded marshes, while in the house, his electric points were below water level. It would take a long, slow, expensive recovery, moving all plug points higher, and a complete paint job was required.

Roger was always walking out, and he always came back – too often at my behest! I have a letter that I sent him after one of his abrupt departures, and here is a resumé:

'Thoughts and thanks: I have drifted through so many happy times that I decided to jot them down – just a small appreciation of a very special 18 months, not always easy, but many personal moments that I hope we can store away for rainy days…

'Trains passing through the Bottle & Kedge; an Irishman in a Suffolk taxi; the first proud outing in the Black Dress with a magnificent escort in a slightly too small dinner shirt; a balmy evening on Sizewell beach; the pile of lobster shells on the first visit to The Swan; a teddy bear and plastic duck in

Cheltenham; a putting course at "Fawlty Towers" – and my favourite moment in a church in Bath.

'It's a good companionship and very personal – don't let people spoil it, and maybe we can find a little time for us.'

Sadly, by the time I got back from South Africa, on top of the flood, both lung cancer and five years of dementia were firmly set in. Surprisingly, Roger became rather affable in his last illness (if still a little difficult) and remained a character that people couldn't help but fall for.

He passed away with his three daughters around him, and I found myself in the same pew as when David died: in the same church and putting on the same wake in the same pub – how bizarre was that?

I look back on Roger with a certain fondness and chuckle that even in his eulogy, it was remarked that he was quite probably asking St Peter if he was hung like a baboon!

My final memory of the day comes as I heard Roger's concerned daughter Sarah exclaim: 'What's she doing now?' For many years, Roger had affectionately called me 'Big Bertha', I assumed because my middle name is Elizabeth. It was only while watching the golf on the telly that I realised Big Bertha was, in fact, a huge oversized golf club designed to go further and enhance players' drives with its giant clout!

To Sarah's astonishment (and many others, no doubt!) I was seen to tap on the departing hearse door and demand it be stopped so I could rummage amongst the flowers. I had decided to attach my wreath of flowers for Roger onto a Big Bertha golf club, pinched from my son-in-law's bag. I panicked a bit when I saw it heading off for the crematorium.

It needed to be retrieved so it could be back, unnoticed, in Tyrone's golf bag before I had another black mark against me!

Typical Roger, getting a good view of the goods!

A wonderful, naughty picture of Roger taken in his latter years.

Arrival of the railway carriages.

*The railway carriages, quirky spare bedrooms, office and potting shed.
Credit: Richard Bloom.*

Shirley, Sarah and Ann, my right-hand ladies! Serving drinks in the Greasy Spoon on garden open days.

Paul, my wonderful gardener, friend and partner in crime in our much-loved garden. Credit: Richard Bloom.

Show Champion! Receiving my trophy at the annual Knodishall Flower Show.

In the honeymoon suite in Mauritius after Roger let me down. A substitute was rapidly found!

CHAPTER 10

Now, I enter the final stages of my life, and as my health gently fades, I look at the way I have chosen to let life take its own course in its own time, foregoing any invasive treatments. I am a firm believer in total positivity, wanting always to give a helping or a listening ear to others who also need help.

It is now more than 20 years since I was first diagnosed with breast cancer. I have had just one operation to remove a year's worth of cysts, and barring dressings, there have been no further treatments.

During lockdown, I joined the wonderful St Elizabeth's Hospice on the outskirts of Ipswich, enabling me to receive their superb support whilst remaining at Priors Oak. With its beautiful tranquil gardens reminiscent in many ways of my own, it is little wonder that several of the Priors Oak Garden family and friends have ended their lives in the wonderful surroundings of the St Elizabeth's unique building and its surroundings.

It was here that I found the anchor and help that I needed to remain positive. I now no longer fear the thought of death, and when the time comes, I know I can take great comfort in the knowledge that St Elizabeth's is there for me. Its basic premise is to help people living with a progressive illness to take back their independence and live the life they have to the full.

The hospice is an independent charity that provides its services free of charge. To do this, it relies heavily on the support and generosity of the local community in East Suffolk. It's constantly developing to meet the needs of people in the local community. It supports more than 2,000 people a year, and the need for their services is growing. St Elizabeth's has, for example, recently developed a young adult group to support young people aged 14 and older with care tailored to their needs.

Each year, it costs almost £13 million to deliver its care services and the running of the organisation, including support in Great Yarmouth and Waveney. Seventy per cent of the hospice's costs have to be raised by fundraising and donations, with just 30 per cent coming from services commissioned by the NHS. This is why I'm totally committed to helping them and finding where I can get the donations they need so much.

I know brain cancer now looms, but I also know I can walk out into my garden and feel this overpowering joy and love that Priors Oak gives me; somehow, Paul and I have achieved the dream we set out to achieve with lots of love and laughter along the way.

Also, I take great pride in knowing that I can now, at last, call myself an Aldeburgh girl! They say it takes 30 years to achieve that status, and as I look across Aldeburgh's big skies, its rolling coast and quaint history, I am truly proud to consider myself part of the furniture. I've spent some of my happiest years here, with marriage in the town, Lucie's birth, forming lifelong friendships with wonderful Suffolk characters, and finally being part of Priors Oak life.

I have no intention of chronicling Aldeburgh's history. Instead, no memoir of my time in this great place would be complete without acknowledging some of the great characters I've met along the way.

From Roy Cartwright restoring our 1930s railway carriages, the endless yarns at Russell's boatyard with Reuben and Jumbo, sailing up and down the Alde on our various boats, and Wilfred, Aldeburgh's pharmacist-turned-local-professional map-maker, keeping Aldeburgh and district accessible to all. And then there are all those characters who head to the old Potty bar on a daily basis to drink and reminisce.

I think of the town's rolling golf course that greets the visitor. And the beach, where legendary fisherman Billy Burrell, David's good friend over the years, kept Lucie in lobsters, as well as my ongoing and long-running friendship with current fishermen Dean, Donna and family. Not forgetting Mike the Moth, who for years opened my moth traps and revealed to me the secret sex life of the moths (not to be sneezed at, let me tell you!) as well as the information stored in owl pellets.

Long may Aldeburgh and all its eccentrics, unique micro-climate and history live on. I am proud to have been a part of it.

And so to the men in my life, many of them known since my teens. I won't name them all, but they know who they are. To them, I say thank you for all the fun, laughter, help and memories over the years, and I send them my love. The Trude knows she's no angel – but she's still flying!

My much-loved garden. Credit: Richard Bloom.

My butterfly meadow, a highlight of my charity open days. Credit: Richard Bloom.

Hard at work with Lucie shortly after my brain cancer diagnosis in 2023.

Trudie, with Lucie and grandchildren Mila and Oli

No angel... just a girl from the Swinging Sixties who's lived her life to the full with love, joy and happiness.

Printed in Great Britain
by Amazon